MARKETING IN THE NEW MEDIA

Holly Berkley

Self-Counsel Press
(a division of)
International Self-Counsel Press Ltd.
USA   Canada

Self-Counsel Press acknowledges the financial support of the Government of Canada through the Book Publishing Industry Development Program (BPIDP) for our publishing activities.

Printed in Canada.

First edition: 2007

Second edition: 2009

Library and Archives Canada Cataloguing in Publication

Berkley, Holly

    Marketing in the new media / Holly Berkley. -- 2nd ed.

ISBN 978-1-55180-872-7

    1. Internet marketing. 2. Internet advertising. 3. Mobile commerce. I. Title.

HF5415.1265B473 2009   658.8'72   C2009-900227-2

Self-Counsel Press
(a division of)
International Self-Counsel Press Ltd.

1704 North State Street	1481 Charlotte Road
Bellingham, WA 98225	North Vancouver, BC V7J 1H1
USA	Canada

CONTENTS

INTRODUCTION   ix

1   AN OVERVIEW OF NEW MEDIA MARKETING   1

Internet Marketing in a Nutshell   3

The Radio Industry's Movement toward New Media   4

Make Your Website the Center of All Your Marketing   5

Combine Traditional Ads with Keyword Buys for
    Maximum Impact   6

    Maximize the effectiveness of keyword phrases   7

    Use every opportunity to generate buzz   8

Rock Star Marketing: Effectively Combining Traditional
    and New Media   9

    Take advantage of co-branding for maximum
        exposure   10

    Use message boards and blogs to generate
        new content   10

    Encourage audience participation   11

    Keep selling   11

    Don't let visitors ignore your advertisers   12

    Use mobile marketing   12

References   13

2	**THE DIGITAL LIFESTYLE**	15
	Internet Usage by Age, Education, and Income Level	16
	What are people doing online?	17
	Using the Internet at work	17
	Using the Internet strictly for fun	18
	The Importance of Social Networking Channels	19
	The Growth of Blogs	19
	Promotion through RSS Advertising	20
	Online Gaming Is Also on the Rise	21
	Who Is Watching Online Video?	21
	A Look at Podcasting	22
	Partnerships in podcasting	24
	Engage Consumers in Your Brand	24
	References	25
3	**JOINING THE CONVERSATION — EXPLORING OPPORTUNITIES ON THE SOCIAL WEB**	27
	Who is Using Social Networking Sites?	30
	Determining the Right Social Networking Approach for Your Business	31
	Engaging the Consumer, Not Selling	32
	Leveraging the Influence of Blogs	33
	Promoting Your Company through Facebook	33
	Choosing between a Facebook Profile, Fan Page, or Group	34
	Buying Social Ads on Facebook	35
	Finding and Managing Your Friends on Facebook	35
	Six Easy Steps for Self-Promotion on Facebook	37
	Getting Your Video Seen on YouTube	38
	Making Friends on MySpace	39
	Getting down to Business on LinkedIn	41
	Brand Ambassadors	41
	Twitter	42
	Find out Who is Talking about You	43

Final Notes on Social Marketing Optimization Strategies   44

References   44

4   WHY USING MOBILE MARKETING NOW IS IMPORTANT   47

Entering the Mobile Marketing Medium   47

Leaders in Mobile Marketing   48

     Mobile marketing and sporting events   50

     Other industries get on board   50

GIS and Mobile Marketing   51

Mobile TV   52

Free Minutes for Mobile Ads   52

Text-to-Win   53

Using Mobile Marketing to Boost Retail Sales   54

Steps for Starting a Mobile Marketing Campaign   55

Customer Respect in Mobile Marketing   57

The Future of Mobile Marketing   58

References   61

5   USING NEW MEDIA TO ENHANCE CUSTOMER SERVICE, TRUST, AND BRAND LOYALTY   63

Creating a Trusted, Branded Personality for Your Site   63

Building Loyalty through Expert Web Content   65

Generating Consumer Trust by Letting Others Do Your Talking   65

Offering Excellent Online Customer Support   66

Staying in the Forefront of Consumers' Minds   67

Using Targeted, Brand-Building Ad Buys   69

Making Your Marketing Message Matter to Your Audience   70

Creating Great Content That Keeps Consumers Coming Back   71

     Creating custom content   72

References   73

**6   DEVELOPING NEW MEDIA CAMPAIGNS BY
      TARGET AUDIENCE AND INDUSTRY**   75

Defining Your Target Audience   75

What Women Look For on the Web   76

Getting to Know Generation Y   78

Targeting Teens and Young Men through Online
   and Mobile Gaming   79

Reaching College Students through Online Social
   Networks   80

Finding Generation X   81

Internet Use by Seniors Is Changing Dramatically   81

Singles Have More Control of Their Time Spent Online   82

Using "Life Stages" to Find New Customers   83

New Media Technology Use by the Auto Industry   84

New Media Marketing in the Travel Industry   87

Nonprofits and Charities: Building a Trustworthy
   Web Presence   90

Local Marketing Strategies with Search Engines   92

When New Media Marketing Is a Must   93

References   94

**7   CONTROLLING YOUR BRAND IMAGE AND PUBLIC
      RELATIONS THROUGH INTERNET MARKETING**   97

The Benefits of Online Press Releases   99

   Creating buzz around your press release   100

   Optimizing your press release for RSS feeds   101

Your Brand, Your Trademark, and the Search Engines   103

Strengthening Your Online Brand through New Media
   Partnerships   104

   Co-branding works when there is synergy   105

   Co-branding guidelines   107

New Branded Television Content   107

Creating Television Shows and Commercials Exclusively
   for New Media Use   109

Making Brand-Building Campaigns Viral   110

References   111

8   IS YOUR WEBSITE READY?   113

Remember the Basics of Good Web Design   113

E-commerce Strategies from Amazon.com   115

The Importance of Easy, Safe Checkout   116

 Consider your audience when providing payment
 options   118

The Right Way to Cross-Sell Online   118

Optimizing Your Website for Search Engines   119

 Search engines read text, not graphics   119

 Choose the right keywords   119

 Your home page and your tags   120

 Text links   123

 Site maps   124

 Frames   124

 Flash pages, image maps, and heavy graphics   124

Link Popularity   125

Is Your Website Ready?   126

How Long Does Getting to the Top Take?   128

Paying for Positioning   129

 Using landing pages   130

 Writing effective ad copy   130

References   131

**9   FINE-TUNING YOUR EMAIL MARKETING
 STRATEGIES**   133

Permission-Based Email Marketing   134

Focus on Content   135

Timing Is Important   136

Write a Great Subject Line   139

Six Easy Steps for Complying with the CAN-SPAM Act   141

The State of Email Marketing   142

References   144

10 MEASURING THE RESULTS   145

Web Traffic Reports   145

Looking at Averages   146

Tracking Delayed or Offline Conversions   146

Can Online Branding Be Measured?   148

Measuring the Success of Search Engine Marketing   149

Measuring the Success of Online PR Efforts   150

Measuring the Success of Mobile Marketing Campaigns   151

Tracking Online Video Results   151

Modifying Your Marketing Campaign Based on Your Results   152

References   153

11 NEXT STEPS: PULLING IT ALL TOGETHER   155

Understand Your Target Audience   155

Identify How You Will Measure the Success of the Campaign   156

Align Your Company Goals and Values to Help Build a Stronger Online Brand   156

Take Time to Plan Your Website   157

Typical Costs for Implementing a New Media Campaign   157

Invest in a Professional Website   158

Search Engine Marketing   159

Testing the Keywords before You Optimize   160

Upselling to Existing Customers through Email Marketing   161

Strategic Partnership Development (Co-Branding)   162

Connecting with the Customer   162

INTRODUCTION

When this book was originally written only a few years ago, business owners and marketing executives were only just starting to realize the power new media marketing strategies could bring to their business. CEOs and company executives were just beginning to step outside their corner offices, take down the corporate walls, and open themselves up to the public on Facebook, LinkedIn, Twitter, and other social media channels. Customer service teams were just starting to leverage new media channels like text messaging, blogs, and live chat to remedy consumer complaints and provide real-time solutions. And marketing directors and creative teams bravely opened the door to their world by allowing actual consumers to create television commercials, submit ideas, and even become brand ambassadors on sites like YouTube.

At the very core, marketing in the new media revolves around catering to today's consumer's demand for control. Control over the information they receive. Control over when they receive that information. And control over how they can respond to it.

Opening yourself and your business up to the public through new media channels can be intimidating and in some cases even frightening! It can mean putting pieces of yourself out there, online for the entire world to see … for good or bad. No matter how daunting it may feel be to get started, participation in the new media world is no longer an option for business owners, it's a requirement. Whether you want them to or not, consumers will be using new media strategies to find information about you, whether they are sharing feedback about your product on an industry blog, or posting a review on their favorite shopping portal. As a business owner or marketing executive, you also want control. And in order to stay in control of your reputation, brand, and messaging, you need to be part of the online conversation.

Throughout this book you will read a few case studies and "lessons learned" from companies that jumped into the new media space without adequate forethought, resulting in some brand-damaging results. However, you will see even more case studies about companies that have leveraged new media successfully ... so successfully, that the efforts literally helped catapult them ahead of their competitors, gain more customers, and in one case, even helped to win the US presidential election in 2008.

Now more than ever marketing teams and business owners understand the importance of seamlessly weaving elements of new media into their marketing mix.

This book provides an introduction to combining traditional and new media effectively to strengthen your company brand. We'll take a close look at case studies that combine television, radio, and/or print marketing with Internet and mobile marketing elements to make a huge impact. We'll look at how you can use Internet marketing to enhance your company image in the public eye (as well as combat any negative publicity). You will also learn elements of successful website design, and how to analyze web traffic reports and online customer behaviors on a deeper level, so you can make informed decisions about how your campaigns are performing and how customers are interacting with your brand. We'll explore how to get a mobile marketing campaign (using SMS — the short messaging service to send text messages via mobile phones or wireless devices) off the ground and explore why big businesses cannot afford to ignore this new "uncluttered" advertising medium.

Finally, in this second edition of *Marketing in the New Media*, you'll see a whole new chapter on social media (see Chapter 3). In this chapter, you'll get insights, case studies, and even a few "lessons learned" on how to leverage yourself, your company, and your brand message through social media channels like Facebook, Twitter, MySpace, YouTube, LinkedIn, and others.

What Defines Traditional versus New Media Advertising Methods?

Throughout this book, when I refer to traditional advertising, I am specially talking about "offline" marketing activities such as radio, television, print ads, billboards, and other outdoor advertising. New media advertising includes promoting your company through new technology such as the web or through mobile devices such as cell phones or iPods.

CHAPTER ONE

AN OVERVIEW OF NEW MEDIA MARKETING

Ever since I can remember, television has been the leader in providing a medium for advertisers to get their messages out to the largest audience in the most effective way possible. However, since the creation of TiVo and other digital video recorder (DVR) technology, advertisers are growing increasingly concerned that viewers are simply skipping their very expensive commercial spots altogether. Combine this with the fact that traditional media channels such as television, radio, and print publications are no longer the only media choices for news and entertainment, and you may find yourself entering some unfamiliar territory to get your marketing message out to your target audience.

Today's new media technology is allowing for more consumer control than ever before, giving the public complete control over what content they see and when they see it. As a result, this change in consumer expectations and media use has forced advertisers to rethink their entire marketing strategy. Big businesses can no longer depend on interruptive marketing tactics such as placing commercials in the middle of your favorite television show. Instead, advertisers have to think strategically about how to incorporate their marketing message into the content that potential customers are actively seeking.

Today, more than 1.4 billion (internetworldstats.com, March 2008) people worldwide are online, tuning in to their favorite websites,

The growing use of TiVo and other DVR technology is forcing advertisers to rethink their marketing strategies.

reading email, chatting online, listening to streaming music, playing games, and downloading videos.

According to a March 2006 study by the Association of National Advertisers and Forrester Research, 78 percent of 133 national advertisers surveyed believe traditional advertising methods have become less effective in the past two years. Of those surveyed, 70 percent believe that the growing use of DVRs and video-on-demand services will further reduce and even destroy the effectiveness of the traditional 30-second television commercial. As a result, overall network spending has declined, while advertisers invest significantly more in Internet advertising opportunities (La Monica, March 2006).

This trend towards new media marketing has forced even the major networks — NBC, CBS, ABC, and FOX — to build an online component into their advertising model in order to keep advertisers happy. All the major networks have now launched online components of their top shows in order to give advertisers a better return on investment — and to give results that can be tracked.

ABC is allowing users to download popular shows such as *Desperate Housewives* and *Lost* the day after they air on prime time. Although the audience may be smaller than those who tune into the larger screen, the new medium is already proving more effective to advertisers who have the opportunity to sponsor the entire online version of the show, as opposed to sharing the more crowded television version which typically includes eight minutes of commercials for a 30-minute show. The other benefit to advertising on the web is that users currently do not have the option to fast-forward through the commercials.

NBC announced they will be tying in custom web-based content with their most popular shows such as *The Office, Law & Order: Criminal Intent*, and *The Tonight Show with Jay Leno*. In addition, they are working on co-branding contests and editorial sections between top websites such as iVillage.com (recently acquired by NBC) with *Today* and *Access Hollywood* (Newcomb, May 2006).

But will users really watch television shows online? As more and more flat screen and high definition televisions enter more homes, advertisers wonder if users will actually download shows to their laptops and home computers.

The answer is yes. Consumers are willing to watch their favorite shows online. In fact, according to Arbitron Internet Media, more than 45 percent of all Americans have listened to audio or watched videos on the Internet at some point. According to the same study, 30 million Americans listen to or watch Internet streams every week.

When CBS streamed more than 15 million live broadcasts of the 2006 March Madness, the sheer numbers proved beyond a doubt that users are willing to view web content online. According to CBS SportsLine, more than 1.3 million people signed up for the free service and visited the site around 5 million times during the NCAA Tournament. The advertisers as well as the network were more than pleasantly surprised by the massive turnout online (La Monica, April 2006a).

However, I want to stress that this book is not simply about buying ads online. Truly effective Internet marketing is not about simply moving a 30-second commercial that was once on television or radio to the web. Internet marketing is much more complex than this. With that said, the complexity of new media should not be seen as an obstacle or intimidate you. Rather, it is a fresh new playing field where almost anything can be tested and implemented — at often a fraction of the cost of traditional media campaigns. This new media opens up exciting new options to reach consumers on a more effective and personal level than ever before. These new forms of marketing are much more accountable, and thus cost-effective, than any other form of advertising.

Internet Marketing in a Nutshell

Online marketing is much more than buying ads online. It's about how you communicate with your customers via email, message boards, chat rooms, and blogs. It is about updating your website with important product information and offers. It is any kind of promotion your company does using the Internet.

Internet marketing also includes using RSS feeds and podcasting to transfer messages over the web. Podcasting refers to the transfer of video or audio files over the Internet to a personal device such as an iPod. RSS feeds, which is an older technology but has recently caught the interest of online PR and marketing experts, allows for easy syndication of information over the Internet and is

Don't settle for banner ads. Get creative, and look for new ways to promote your brand message online.

often used on news websites (more about RSS feeds and online PR in Chapter 7). Understanding the benefits, opportunities, and limitations of new media technology helps you to more effectively market your brand and gain increased access to your intended audience.

The Radio Industry's Movement toward New Media

Last week I had a meeting with an ad rep from Clear Channel Radio to discuss the new online opportunities they were offering for advertisers. I was disappointed when the presentation largely consisted of banner ads that ran on their radio station websites or alongside streaming radio programs. I pushed the rep a bit further, asking, "Why would I recommend a banner ad on one of your websites, when online marketing options such as pay-per-click are a quarter of the cost and already proven effective?" Although the rep did mention an opportunity to sponsor an original podcast and was open to doing some custom campaigns with me, he admitted that he did not yet have any case studies, rates, or advertisers willing to commit to the newer media opportunities. Most companies considering moving advertising dollars online felt more comfortable with something a bit more familiar, such as banner ads.

I then realized that the radio industry is experiencing many of the same problems as television, with advertisers looking for more new media components for their messages. And like television, most radio executives aren't quite sure how to combine new and traditional media advertising. However, along with the sales pack, I was given a list of impressive stats proving the effectiveness of advertising on online radio. For example, during a one-week study in 2004, 19 million Americans (8 percent of the US population) listened to online radio. The same group also reported that Internet radio is their soundtrack for online shopping — more than 42 percent of people who listen to Internet radio do so while buying or researching a product or service online.

Given these impressive stats on Internet radio use (and similar stats for online video), why are so many major advertisers so slow to take advantage of new media opportunities? The fact is, new media is still growing, and both advertisers and media giants are continuing to test what works. With new technology constantly evolving, there will always be new ways to generate consumer interest through new media.

Rather than overwhelm you with all the new marketing trends emerging almost daily, this book was written to give you insight into the basics of Internet marketing and the absolutely essential elements that must be incorporated into your traditional campaigns to give you maximum return on investment.

Make Your Website the Center of All Your Marketing

The first key to effective new media advertising is your website. Your website should be the center of all your advertising efforts. Sending users to your website to claim a coupon or take advantage of a promotion allows you, as the marketer, a direct way to track which advertising channel is most cost-effective and provides the best results. It also allows you to track your messages, promotions, and ad buys more accurately than in any other medium. This gives you the information you need to refine your media and messages as needed.

The design of your website is essential to the success of your marketing efforts, as this is often the final step to close the lead and capture a user's information in some way. The feelings consumers have when they visit your website carry over to how they perceive your entire company or organization. It is essential that all of your marketing efforts, both traditional and new, are in sync and offer the same branding message across all platforms. No matter how effective your marketing campaign is, if you don't have a well-designed, professional-looking website, people will not buy from you. (See Chapters 4 and 7 for more about ensuring your website is ready for a new media campaign.)

Using your website as the center of your marketing also allows you to interact with consumers on a much more personal level than other forms of marketing. The producers of the popular ABC television show *Lost* have set up a website not only to promote the show but also as a way for writers and marketers to essentially listen to what fans are saying about the show — and make changes accordingly. Allowing users to freely post comments on message boards is a great way to generate honest feedback about your product, so you can know what elements to tweak to make it even better.

On an interview posted on a fan website Lost-TV.com, creator and executive producer Damon Lindeloff said, "The fan reaction has a LOT of influence ... the biggest example is that we began to sense

Updating a web page is much faster and cheaper than altering a television or print piece. Use your website to test new promotions before they go to print or video.

Buy keyword phrases that relate to your television commercials. If you don't, your competitors will!

the real frustration from fans that we weren't answering any questions and just asking new ones ... [So we] gave the audience more answers than we were originally planning to" (Parker, April 2006).

Although opening up your product or service (or in this case a television show) to your audience's honest feedback is a great market research tool, be careful. Make sure your message boards and chat rooms are monitored on a continual basis so you can keep some control over what is posted. After all, you don't want visitors posting derogatory or negative things that may affect your public image. And while customer feedback from websites may encourage you to modify your product or service, don't let visitors control your brand. (Even the writers of *Lost* allowed only certain staff members to see the viewer comments, to make sure the entire show didn't get skewed in the wrong direction.)

Combine Traditional Ads with Keyword Buys for Maximum Impact

The importance of directing potential customers to one's website was proven during the 2006 Super Bowl. During the game, top companies spent more than $200 million with ABC to showcase their brands, but only 40 percent mentioned a website. The companies that not only mentioned their website but also made sure they had top search rankings for their product keywords reaped the most benefits.

Companies ensure high rankings on top search engines by having their website professionally optimized for specific keyword phrases (more about how to optimize your website in Chapter 7). However, those major brands that wanted immediate control over top placement and messaging simply purchased keyword phrases on top search engines such as Google and Yahoo!. Also known as PPC or pay-per-click advertising, this is a highly effective way to ensure your marketing message is up to date and at the top of search engine results.

Just days before and after the 2006 Super Bowl, Yahoo! reported an 800 percent increase in searches for Super Bowl ad-related terms (comScore Networks, February 2006). Companies that included an online video version of their Super Bowl commercials reaped the benefits of having their commercials viewed again and again. They also benefited from the Internet's most powerful marketing tool — viral or word-of-mouth marketing — as many online commercials were forwarded to friends via email, blogs, or message boards. (More about social networks and word-of-mouth marketing in Chapter 2.)

Other companies simply made sure their brands appeared at the top of these high-volume searches. These companies included Cadillac, Honda, and Dove, which according to Yahoo! all bid on the time-appropriate phrase "Super Bowl XL Commercials" on Yahoo! Search and took advantage of the resulting increase in search traffic.

Cadillac must know that 70 percent of today's auto buyers research online before visiting a dealer because Cadillac made sure to buy keywords related to their cars, specifically the Cadillac Escalade, which was featured during the Super Bowl. Yahoo! reported that searches for the car increased over 75 percent just after the Super Bowl ad appeared, and traffic to the Cadillac site increased by 250 percent (comScore Networks, February 2005).

Ford, on the other hand, severely missed out by not purchasing related keywords after their Super Bowl ad aired promoting the new Escape Hybrid starring Kermit the Frog. In fact, this oversight led not only to missed traffic, it actually helped their competitors! GM purchased the word "Kermit" to promote their own hybrid car line, getting the targeted traffic from Ford's Super Bowl ad without the huge costs!

Maximize the effectiveness of keyword phrases

Even if your company is not a specific advertiser in a major event such as the Super Bowl, thinking of phrases users may be searching for around a specific holiday or event can help you find access to new customers. For example, during the 2006 Super Bowl there was more than a 100 percent increase in searches for "appetizer recipes," "salsa," and "chicken wings." If you own a local restaurant that delivers, or a catering service, or any company that can benefit from this or related keywords, you can put your company ad in front of a target audience without having to spend hundreds of thousands of dollars.

Clearly the biggest winners in the Super Bowl XXXIX ad campaigns were the dot-coms. They understood the power of the Internet in measuring ad success and encouraging customer interaction with brands.

CareerBuilder.com, GoDaddy.com, and Overstock.com all complemented their Super Bowl television ads with keywords buys and landing pages that rewarded users for visiting their websites after the game.

According to comScore Networks, Go Daddy's "wardrobe malfunction" ad campaign proved most successful, shooting their traffic up 1,564 percent after the Super Bowl ad, achieving more than 439,000 unique visitors for one day. The controversial company played on the fact that their first rounds of commercials were not suitable for air on ABC, and specifically told audiences to "see more coverage at GoDaddy.com." This direct call to action helped Go Daddy achieve more Internet traffic than any of the other top brands that purchased five times more airtime than Go Daddy (comScore Networks, February 2006).

Use every opportunity to generate buzz

Not only did some advertisers miss the opportunity to benefit from search engine and website presence following the Super Bowl, the television shows that followed also missed out on a chance to generate longer term buzz.

Grey's Anatomy is the television show that followed the Super Bowl. Although I am an avid watcher of the medical dramedy, I was a bit shocked by the very steamy opening shower scene that appeared just after the Super Bowl. In fact, I was a bit embarrassed when my husband's friend announced, "THIS is the show you watch every Sunday night!" At first I thought the show had taken a turn for the worse, but then I realized the opening scene was a great marketing ploy to get the attention of the men in the room, who may previously have considered *Grey's Anatomy* a "girly" show.

The episode really drew in the new audience and kept everyone at the edge of their seats. However, the show missed out on capturing that audience even further because it did not purchase specific keywords that had to do with the show and therefore failed to get the new audience even more hooked. After the episode, searches for "Grey's Anatomy" increased roughly 400 percent on Yahoo!, while the search phrase "code black," referring to a mysterious event in the show, jumped over 1,000 percent.

If you go to the *Grey's Anatomy* website (through ABC at http://abc.go.com/primetime/greysanatomy/), you will notice that like most television shows, they are taking advantage of new media opportunities such as ringtones, music downloads, DVD sales, blogs, and other interactive content to really get their audience hooked. They even have a list of all the diseases and medical problems mentioned on the show — with links to related sources.

Although the site is professionally designed and employs some cutting-edge design technology (for example, clicking on the character bios lets you actually flip through their files on a clipboard), it can feel like information overload. Even to someone like me, who is a fan of the show and Internet technology, there is simply too much information on this site. It seems they added *all* the new media elements for the sake of adding them. I consider this overkill — and not very effective.

Creating an interesting and interactive web presence for your company, service, or show is essential, but it's also important to have a good reason for adding those online elements. Never use technology for the sake of technology. There must be a reason that makes sense for your target audience and provides something useful to them. With that said, below is an example of a show that captured all the elements of Internet marketing to create ongoing excitement and buzz around their show.

Rock Star Marketing: Effectively Combining Traditional and New Media

The concept behind the 2005 reality show *Rock Star: INXS* was nothing new. Put a group of 15 strangers in a house together, make them compete, and then eliminate them one by one until you're left with the next lead signer of INXS. Think of it as *Survivor* meets *American Idol*, but with an edge.

I have to admit that I am one of the few people left who never watches reality TV. So the fact that I got hooked on this reality show made me think about the marketing elements involved and why I couldn't get it out of my head.

It all started one Monday morning when I logged onto MSN.com (which is my default home page on my computer). Right there on the top of the page was an animated banner promoting *Rock Star: INXS*. That night, when I started seeing promotions on TV that matched the banner, I became interested. I watched the

New technology and website content should help enhance your brand — not distract from it.

first episode, was entertained, but didn't get hooked right away. It wasn't until the next morning when I started up my computer again, and there it was, right on the home page of MSN — a recap of the show, plus all kinds of clickable online marketing elements that took me deeper into the show and its characters, music, and energy.

There was nothing low budget about CBS's co-branding with MSN. They spared no expense, including all the best elements of online marketing, all in one spot: RockStar.MSN.com. (Although there was also information about *Rock Star: INXS* on CBS.com, this site did not draw you in and make you come back for more the way MSN's did.)

Below is a list of online marketing elements from RockStar.MSN.com, along with a brief look at how incorporating similar features can maximize your next campaign.

Take advantage of co-branding for maximum exposure

CBS co-branded their reality show with one of the biggest properties on the web, MSN, and partnered with an already established, well-known rock band, INXS. Between the two brands, the show was off to a strong start, with built-in credibility and reach (MSN technology and traffic) and existing interest (the INXS fan base).

Co-branding works when all parties involved benefit from the partnership. MSN and INXS benefited from the television exposure, while CBS benefited from the technological resources and huge exposure MSN provides to the online world. It was a win-win situation for all parties.

Use message boards and blogs to generate new content

Click on any of the *Rock Star: INXS* contestants' profile pages and you could find their personal blogs about the previous night's performances, and read their random thoughts and about their latest fears. There was also a message board so fans can ask questions and give feedback.

Blogs are an efficient way to keep content fresh and keep the audience coming back for more. But generating new content for your website every day or every week can require a tremendous amount of resources. Whenever you can, have your customers (or in this case, the viewers and the contestants) generate content on your website. It also helps make the site interesting as well as sincere.

Encourage audience participation

Rock Star: INXS was not the first television show to ask the audience to log in to their website or to send a text message to cast their votes. However, this media campaign is worth mentioning here because it is the ultimate way to create synergy between an offline and an online campaign.

The same idea works with any type of contest or special information that your audience can only get online. The benefits of pushing an offline audience online is that you are then able to track their behavior in far more detail than you could with traditional advertising. Once you get a customer to your website, you can really monitor their activities and find out what they are most interested in. In this case, CBS and MSN can tell which contestants get the most views, what songs get downloaded most often, and how the audience feels about the show in general (by reviewing the message boards). You just can't get this type of detail about audiences or customers from television marketing alone.

Keep selling

Any well-thought-out promotional website has an element of e-commerce. You used to be able to log on to RockStar.MSN.com, pull out your credit card, and start browsing through all the songs from the show, available for $0.99 each exclusively through the MSN Music store. Here you could purchase and download songs performed by your favorite contestant as well as the version performed by the original artist. You could also click on the "Store" link to view all of the INXS products you could possibly want.

Throughout both the music download area and INXS products area, you could easily click over to more general MSN shopping areas, making this the perfect gateway to keep visitors moving through all channels of MSN. Or, you could pop over to iTunes and download the latest versions of JD Fortune's "Pretty Vegas" to your iPod.

Encouraging offline audiences to interact with your website gives you more insight into how they feel about your brand.

Don't let visitors ignore your advertisers

If you forgot to record an episode of *Rock Star: INXS* on TiVo, or just wanted to see your favorite contestants perform again, you could download the videos online. However, don't think this gets you out of seeing the television commercials that come with the show. As I downloaded the Week Two performance of Daphna, I had to watch a 30-second Honda commercial first. No fast-forwarding allowed. After all, it's advertisers like Honda that are footing the bill for all this.

Use mobile marketing

No cutting-edge marketing campaign is complete without involving mobile marketing in some way. CBS teamed up with Verizon Wireless to offer such gimmicks as INXS ringtones, wallpapers, and phone video clips. Along with some very targeted banner ads and well-designed landing pages, it incorporated many elements that encouraged fans to keep clicking.

The *Rock Star: INXS* online marketing campaign contained all the elements that make me excited about being an online marketer. Whether it's co-branding with other web properties, hosting creative blogs, or providing targeted music downloads, the campaign has something to encourage every fan to get hooked, tell friends about it, and log on for more.

This campaign is just one example of how one brand successfully combined elements of both traditional and new media marketing to make a powerful impact. Keep reading to learn more about what types of new media elements attract what type of audience and how to ensure that your marketing message is delivered to the right audience, at the right time, in the most effective way possible.

References

Carton, Sean. 2006. Converging TV and Online through the Mouse. *ClickZ*, April 17.

comScore Networks. 2005. Super Bowl Ad Campaigns Send Viewers Rushing to the Web. February 8.

____. 2006. Super Bowl Ad Campaigns Spike Web Traffic. February 7.

DiGuido, Al. 2006. Marketing Budget Allocation: Follow the Money. *ClickZ*, April 6.

Evans, Dave. 2006. Ad-Skipping Controls: Phillips Has It Right. *ClickZ*, April 26.

Internet World Stats. 2008. World Internet Usage and Population Statistics. www.internetworldstats.com/stats.htm

La Monica, Paul R. 2006. To Be on TV or Not to Be on TV. *CNNMoney.com*, March 27.

____. 2006a. Free TV: Stream It and They Will Come. *CNNMoney.com*, April 3.

____. 2006b. Online Video: Must-free TV. *CNNMoney.com*, April 10.

Lerma, Pete. 2006. Making the Switch. *ClickZ*, April 4.

Newcomb, Kevin. 2006. NBC Ties Fall Schedule to Online Content. *ClickZ*, May 16.

Parker, Pamela. 2006. The Revolution Is Being Televised. *ClickZ*, April 7.

CHAPTER TWO
THE DIGITAL LIFESTYLE

The digital lifestyle is all around us, and it reaches all corners of the world in some way. A few years ago, my husband and I traveled to Dublin, Ireland, and all the way to Mexico City to see U2. With my Verizon Pocket PC cell phone in hand, I could stay connected to the office back in San Diego, California, at all times. In fact, most clients didn't even realize I was out of the office. Along the way, we used the phone to snap photos and capture videos of our travels (as well as of Bono, of course!). We stayed in touch via text messages with our friends without having to pay long distance telephone charges.

Every night of the concert, in every city of the tour, Bono asked the audience to pull out their cell phones and send a text message to make a difference in his ONE campaign. No matter how many times I saw this, I was still amazed that almost every person in the audience had a glowing cell phone to help light up the night. Such a long way from when people held up cigarette lighters at concerts! Bono told his audiences that we had the tools to make a difference and have our voices heard. That power was right in our hands.

The idea of power in consumers' hands is a key component to marketing in the new media and the basis behind the continued growth and evolution of the digital lifestyle. Successful new media marketing has two primary goals: to reach a very targeted audience

Understanding how your target audience uses new media technology will help you develop the most effective marketing plan to reach them.

at the right time, when they are most likely to take an intended action, and to encourage the growing trend towards consumer control of media and content. Targeting, timing, and true consumer-generated media (CGM) are what make all the elements I describe throughout this book work effectively.

Internet Usage by Age, Education, and Income Level

So, who exactly do new media marketing strategies target? Well, almost everyone, actually. According to Pew Internet & American Life Project, more than 400 million people globally are online (Madden, April 2006). In the US alone, more than 172 million people (77 percent of the adult population) are regular Internet users according to a Harris Interactive poll (*eMarketer*, May 2006f).

There is a direct correlation between higher education/higher income and using the Internet more frequently. For example, the Internet Penetration and Impact report by Pew/Internet found that 91 percent of college graduates regularly go online while only 40 percent of adults with less than a high school education do so. As income level rises, so does the likelihood of having an Internet connection at home and using it frequently. Households with an annual income of less than $30,000 are only 53 percent likely to be online, while households with income between $30,000 and $50,000 are 80 percent likely to be online. And that percentage continues to increase as income level rises (Madden, April 2006).

Another important statistic for marketers to consider is that about 84 million Americans have broadband connection in their homes. That is almost double the number from the previous year. This growing number of high speed Internet connections allows marketers to get much more creative with their online promotions, which were once limited by file size and slow downloads with dial-up connections.

Breaking down the Internet usage numbers even further, by age group, shows that nearly everyone is an active part of the digital lifestyle (Madden, April 2006). Here are the current statistics:

- 12–17-year-olds: 87 percent online

- 18–29-year-olds: 88 percent online

- 30–49-year-olds: 84 percent online

- 50–64-year-olds: 71 percent online

- 65+ years old: 32 percent online

(See Chapter 5 for more details on ways to reach these specific target audiences and how different demographic segments differ in their use of new media technology.)

What are people doing online?

So what are all of these millions of people doing online? According to a February to April 2006 Pew/Internet survey (representing 143 million Americans), users are spending 91 percent of their online time reading and sending emails, followed by using search engines or map sites. Seventy-nine percent of users are looking up health and medical information, followed by 78 percent of people researching products, services, weather, hobby information, or travel information. Sixty-eight percent of users are getting news online (Madden, April 2006).

Shopping is another primary activity for Internet users, whether directly purchasing a product over the Internet or researching a product before they buy offline. A study from Shop.org, conducted by Forrester Research, projects that online sales will exceed $200 billion in 2006 (*eMarketer*, May 2006d). Internet marketing and well-designed websites allow retailers to consistently find more than one-third of their new customers. Most often, online consumers are purchasing travel-related items, including airline tickets, vacation packages, and hotel accommodation. The next largest industry categories of online sales include computer hardware and software, automobiles, clothing, and footwear. Pet supplies, cosmetics, and fragrances are expected to see growth rates of 30 percent in 2006, exceeding any other categories. (We'll take a look at the best ways to market to consumers in each of these industry categories, as well as others, in Chapter 6.)

Using the Internet at work

During the workday, the average employee spends about 13 hours per week accessing the Internet, 24 percent of which is spent visiting non-work-related sites. So where are all these workers going on company time? According to the seventh annual Web@Work study from Websense, conducted by Harris Interactive, top sites include

Today's corporate decision makers say that the Internet is the best way to reach them.

map sites, news, and weather. These findings were consistently reported by both employees and IT managers who monitored staff Internet usage; however, as you get further down the list of non-work-related sites, the numbers start to conflict. For example, 3 percent of employees admit visiting dating sites, while IT managers found the number is actually closer to 18 percent. And while less than 1 percent admit visiting gambling or sex sites while at work, IT managers found those stats average 10 percent (*eMarketer*, May 2006c).

Now that we know what the average employee is doing online, what about the upper-level executives, business owners, and key decisions makers in the company? According to a 2002 survey conducted by Nielsen//NetRatings and the *Washington Post*, 77 percent of key business decision makers believe that the Internet is the absolute best place to find out about new products. Sixty-six percent recommend online advertising as the best way to reach them. That is higher than magazines, newspapers, radio, and even television! By using the web to market your product, you have the opportunity to put your product in front of the most demographically desirable customers during the web's prime time — the business day, when consumers are more likely to take action and less likely to be distracted by other forms of media.

The study found that the Internet is not only the most used medium during the workday, but over 90 percent of executives who use the Internet regularly at work log on from home as well. This makes Internet use during the evening and late hours second only to television viewing.

Using the Internet strictly for fun

On any given day, 40 million Internet users go online just for fun, to pass the time (Fallows, February 2006). Men are typically more likely to "hang out" online with no particular goal, while women users tend to be a bit more goal oriented. Also, the younger the web user, the more likely they are to go online strictly for fun. Other determining factors in web usage for fun are Internet experience and home broadband access. Thirty-six percent of those Internet users with more than six years of Internet experience will surf the Internet for no particular reason, and also 72 percent of those with home broadband Internet connections will use the web in this way.

The Importance of Social Networking Channels

Surfing the web for fun often leads users to get involved in the fastest growing online phenomenon: social networking. In the past few years, online social networking has become a core component to a successful new media strategy, which is why in this second edition of *Marketing in the New Media* I have dedicated a new chapter to this topic. Skip to Chapter 3 for Social Media Optimization (SMO) strategies to help leverage your company, brand, or message on top social sites like YouTube, Facebook, Twitter, Digg, MySpace, LinkedIn, and more.

The Growth of Blogs

Donald Trump has a blog. So do Michael Moore and Ariana Huffington, as well as thousands of celebrities, musicians, business executives, and average people. Blogs (also called "weblogs") provide a way for nontechnical people to post information about their personal lives, beliefs, politics, businesses, products, services, or anything else in a chronological, diary-type format. Many blogs allow visitors to provide feedback on those comments as well.

Since 2003, the growth rate of blogs has doubled about every six months, reaching 35.3 million in April 2006. According to Technorati (http://technorati.com), a blog tracking site, the Internet world sees an average of 1.6 million legitimate blog posts every day, many posts related to new product announcements and scheduled events (Burns, April 2006b).

Blogs are an important marketing tool for your business for many reasons. First, they allow you to develop a closer connection with customers, to generate feedback, and to provide customer support. For an example of a corporate blog, take a look at GM Blogs (www.gmblogs.com) — the General Motors home for their corporate blogs.

The second reason blogs are an important piece of marketing is because they are a great way to help increase search engine ranking for your site. Because blogs are largely text based, they are easy for search engines to index. And because every entry includes a date and search engines look to post the most recently updated site first, your blog has a good chance of ranking high. If your blog entry contains relevant keywords, a recent date, and links to more pages of

Almost half of all web users participate on some type of social networking site. In 2006, MySpace was the second most visited site on the net!

your website, you have a good chance of increasing your ranking. Likewise, because blogs open products up to consumer feedback and word-of-mouth marketing, you are more likely to find both media and consumers referring to and linking back to your blog, which provides added points to increase your search ranking.

However, despite the impressive growth of blogs, corporate blogs still account for only a small percentage of the current blogosphere. Although many executives realize their importance, they are either unsure of how to make blogs work effectively for their company or they simply lack the time and energy to keep a corporate blog updated and running (Burns, May 2006). (More about corporate blogging and how it can enhance your brand and consumer trust in Chapters 3 and 7.)

Promotion through RSS Advertising

Journalists and reporters for media outlets, both traditional and new, are definitely an important segment of the digital lifestyle. Thanks to the growth of RSS feeds for easy syndication of online news, journalists now rely on new media channels more than phone or fax as a means of generating fresh content. (RSS allows users to access and be alerted of content that is frequently updated.) In fact, more than 92 percent of journalists working at newspapers, magazines, and broadcasting outlets nationwide use the Internet for article research, and 81 percent of those journalists search online daily (Crowell, June 2004). (More about how to reach online journalists in Chapter 7.)

RSS technology has been traditionally used by news professionals to syndicate content online primarily by organizations such as Reuters, CNN, PR Newswire, Business Wire, and the BBC. These providers allowed other websites to incorporate their headlines or headline-and-short-summary feeds under various usage agreements. Today, anyone with a website, blog, press release, product announcement, or other marketing promotion can benefit from RSS technology, and because there are so many niche content sources now available, using RSS feeds to send out targeted content is an excellent way to get results. RSS feeds are proving more effective to advertisers than email marketing because it is such a new and uncrowded medium. (More about RSS advertising and how to implement an effective online PR campaign in Chapter 7.)

Online Gaming Is Also on the Rise

Another new media marketing opportunity that is growing involves online gaming. As of April 2006, 31 percent of American Internet users are playing online games (according to Pew/Internet), and in-game advertising is quickly becoming one of the top advertising choices of the new media marketer (Fallows, February 2006). According to the Yankee Group, the ad budget spent on this medium drastically increases every year, with $732 million expected to be spent annually by 2010 (Burns, April 2006a).

And online gaming isn't just for teens. I often find my 35-year-old husband logging on to his favorite video games in the late hours of the night, to compete online with his former college buddies who are scattered throughout California. They'll have an instant messenger going alongside the game, so they can "talk smack" or just catch up on old times during a little friendly competition.

My husband and his friends are definitely not alone out there in the world of cybergaming. According to an Associated Press-AOL Games Poll, 40 percent of Americans play video games, and 45 percent of those play them online. The study also found that while men play more games online than women, they also use the online gaming more socially than women. While women tend to play games solo, men often play online with others. Since 41 percent of gamers play three to four hours per week, they are probably reducing their television viewing (*eMarketer*, May 2006b). This could be one of the major reasons why one in three people born after 1980 can't name the TV networks (Evans, May 2006b).

Who Is Watching Online Video?

Online video is quickly become a standard part of the new media experience. As discussed in Chapter 1, a primary way the television industry is attempting to market its new shows to media-savvy audiences is through online video. While both men and women watch online video files, a study by comScore Networks found that males are much more engaged, watching an average of 120 minutes per month, while females watch 80 minutes per month. Males aged 25 to 34 make up the most dedicated viewers, averaging 140 minutes per month. These numbers represent an 18 percent increase from October 2005 to March 2006, showing that online video use is continuing to grow (*eMarketer*, May 2006e).

Keeping an updated blog can help increase your search engine ranking and overall online exposure. However, only a small percentage of businesses currently use blogs.

As more brands enter the new media market space, we will see more sophisticated video campaigns emerge. In other words, as the new media market space matures, advertisers will have to do more than simply posting television shows or commercials on the web. With so much creative and innovative content to choose from, Internet users will be looking for videos with more value — whether it's education, humor, or simply original entertainment. As the novelty of online videos wears off, consumers need more motivation to seek out an online video or share it with friends. As marketers, if you can put together the right combination of originality, humor, and entertainment, the marketing potential of that video can be absolutely viral.

An original online video is what launched the US band OK Go! into instant stardom. It all started when the band was practicing a dance routine in a modest Chicago backyard for the song "A Million Ways." Rather than practicing in a real dance studio, with such luxuries as a full-length mirror, the band set up a video camera to record their routine. The resulting video was absolutely hilarious! A girlfriend of one of the band members thought the practice video was so amusing that she insisted they use it as their real video. The band laughed. She was serious. As the story goes, she then stole the video, emailed it to a few friends, and 2.5 million downloads later, the band was asked to perform on *The Tonight Show* and *Good Morning America.* They eventually made their way to the MTV Music Video Awards to perform a reenactment of their follow-up video, "Here It Goes Again," better known as the "treadmill song."

As with any marketing plan, the goal of using new media elements should be the same as when using traditional marketing methods — to increase sales or market share. In the case of OK Go!'s viral videos, it definitely led to more direct sales. As a result of the 7 million downloads of the treadmill video for "Here It Goes Again," the band's album quickly became one of the top 100 on iTunes with a top 100 song. If you haven't yet seen either of the OK Go! videos, it's well worth a click over to YouTube to witness firsthand what all the talk is about. I guarantee you'll mention the video to at least a few friends afterward!

A Look at Podcasting

Podcasting, a term originally derived from Apple's mobile music player the iPod, is a way of distributing and sharing multimedia files such as audio and video files over the web. The files can then be downloaded to a personal computer or mobile device such as an iPod. In this discussion I am not referring to commercial music downloads from sites such as iTunes, but specifically about content such as news clips, radio shows, and very targeted content made available via podcasting technology.

With less than 1 percent of Americans listening to such podcasts, the stats are less impressive than for online gaming, social networks, video downloads, or Internet usage in general. However, this does not mean this new media channel should be ignored. In fact, Forrester projects podcasting will reach 12.3 million households by 2010, although primarily reaching an audience of educated males with high average income as well as youth audiences seeking music, entertainment, and tech info (Lieb, May 2006).

Although fewer people regularly download and listen to podcasts, this medium still allows marketers to get their message to a highly targeted and engaged audience. If you choose to use podcasting as a way to get your message out, here are some points to consider:

1. **Consider your business goals and brand**

   Create content that not only reinforces your brand, but is also interesting and useful to the customer. Consider your overall business goals and what you hope your podcast will achieve, whether that is establishing yourself as a leader in the field by providing important information, enhancing your credibility, increasing media attention through increased exposure to a niche group, or driving direct sales.

2. **Make your podcast easily available**

   Making sure your podcast is accessible via search engines and primary portals where people seek podcast content is essential to success. Make your podcast available to search engine spiders by including text-based descriptions detailing the content of your podcast, so both users and search engines will know what your podcast is about before they click. Make your podcast available on top podcasting portals such as Odeo, Yahoo! Podcasts, and Podcast.net.

More brands are thinking about incorporating advergaming into their new media marketing mix. Visit BKGamer.com for a look at Burger King's latest Xbox game.

Although the number of people who download non-music-related podcasts is still relatively small, this technology allows you to reach a very targeted and engaged audience.

3. **Promote your podcast**

   Mention your podcasts in your traditional advertising, post links on your website, and promote the content in your newsletters. It's also a good idea to create a blog or message board around your podcast to encourage feedback.

4. **Promote complementary podcasts**

   Similar to the idea of link exchanges, promoting other podcasts that will in turn promote yours helps everyone involved by opening up your content to a wider audience and establishing credibility.

Partnerships in podcasting

For some companies, the idea of sponsoring an existing podcast is much more appealing that taking the time to develop one on your own. For example in 2006, Travelocity teamed up with a leading travel personality, Rick Steves. He had already built up a large following through his more traditional outlets of guidebooks, radio shows, and television. When he took his show online in the form of podcasting, it seemed like a natural match for Travelocity. Keep in mind that even for personalities like Rick Steves and large companies like Travelocity, this is a new medium (Lerma, May 2006). So prices for sponsorship and how the partnership will work are often completely open to negotiation by both parties.

My suggestion is to take a look at already existing top podcasters related to your industry, and then start a dialogue. Be ready to propose how you think the partnership could work and how much you'd like to pay as a starting point, since most podcasters really have no idea what to charge sponsors.

Engage Consumers in Your Brand

I'd like to emphasize again that new media differ from any of the traditional media channels in that consumers are actively engaged in the media and seeking out information. New media marketing is less interruptive, more targeted, and relies on a person's genuine need to socialize and to seek and share information. Compared to letting content of television and radio come to them, Internet users are actively engaged and more likely to take direct action when they see your marketing message. This is not to say the traditional media are ineffective; in fact, I am suggesting quite the opposite. In order to create a successful campaign, you can no longer choose new media *or* traditional advertising campaigns — you must work to incorporate both.

Here is an example: a March 2006 survey by Burst Media found that nearly half of consumers said television most effectively captures their attention, but those same consumers admitted that when it comes to actually making a decision to purchase a product or service, the Internet ranked first. They went so far as to say that the Internet was their *primary* source for this information (*eMarketer*, May 2006a).

As you read this book, remember that the key to combining traditional and new media marketing is not only about exposing your brand to your target audience, but about truly engaging the consumer, by encouraging them to take action and become more loyal to your product.

Because podcasting is so new, the terms for sponsoring a podcast are often open for negotiation.

References

Bausch, Suzy, and Leilani Han. 2006. Social Networking Sites from 47 Percent, Year over Year, Reaching 45 Percent of Web Users, According to Nielsen//NetRatings. Nielsen//NetRatings, May 11.

Blackshaw, Pete. 2006. Skype Nation. *ClickZ*, May 30.

Burns, Enid. 2006a. In-Gaming Advertising to Continue Exponential Growth. *ClickZ*, April 17.

____. 2006b. Blogosphere Doubles Every Six Months. *ClickZ*, April 18.

____. 2006. Executives Slow to See Value of Corporate Blogging. *ClickZ*, May 9.

Crowell, Grant. 2004. Public Relations via Search Engines. *ClickZ*, June 30.

eMarketer. 2006a. When Americans Buy … They Go Online First, May 2.

____. 2006b. Video Games Entice 4 out of 10 Americans, May 17.

____. 2006c. Where Do Workers Go Online?, May 24.

____. 2006d. Online Retail Predicted to Top $200 Billion, May 25.

____. 2006e. Who's Not Watching Online Video?, May 26.

____. 2006f. Poll Shows 77% of US Adults Are Now Online, May 30.

Evans, Dave. 2006a. Interruptive Media: Just Say No. *ClickZ*, May 10.

____. 2006b. The Power of 'And' in your Media Mix. *ClickZ*, May 24.

Fallows, Deborah. 2006. Browsing the Web for Fun. Pew Internet & American Life Project, February.

Kingdon, Mark. 2006. Social Networking Is Your Friend. *ClickZ*, April 11.

Lieb, Rebecca. 2006. whyPod? *Clickz*, May 26.

Lerma, Pete. 2006. No Formulas for Podcast Sponsorships. *ClickZ*, May 30.

Madden, Mary. 2006. Internet Penetration and Impact. Pew Internet & American Life Project, April.

Newcomb, Kevin. 2006. Sisterwoman Promises Social Networking Without the Risk. *ClickZ*, April 20.

Rodgers, Zachary. 2006. New Social Site Tries for 'MomSpace.' *ClickZ*, May 10.

CHAPTER THREE
JOINING THE CONVERSATION — EXPLORING OPPORTUNITIES ON THE SOCIAL WEB

It was September, 2008. My husband and I just finished watching the Republican National Convention on a major television network. All the reporters and Republican hosts were patting themselves on the back for the great speech Sarah Palin gave, and thinking what a great choice it was to award her the Republican Vice Presidential nomination. Only moments later, I got an invitation to join the latest Facebook Group, "Sarah Palin is NOT Hillary Clinton."

Shortly after, I was invited to join "I have more Foreign Policy Experience than Sarah Palin." Although both groups were, at the time, less than one week old, they each had more than 15,000 members and were quickly growing.

While Republicans continued to praise themselves on traditional media like TV, radio, and even in the issue of Newsweek with Sarah Palin & John McCain on the cover, (the feature article showing Sarah Palin proudly holding up a giant salmon with the headline "McCain's Mrs. Right,") the real conversation about what the actual public thought and felt about the 2008 presidential campaign was happening in new media, primarily on the social web.

From the user-generated YouTube videos, Facebook groups, viral emails, blogs, and personal websites, the public was creating their own support for their favorite presidential candidate — and doing so in a powerful way.

Although the viral momentum of Barack Obama's campaign was a result of the public quickly sharing information through the social web, the campaign itself was no accident. Obama's new media marketing strategy was extremely thought out, deliberately seeded, and well funded. Several reports have estimated that the Obama campaign invested more than $8 million in its online marketing efforts. A large price tag, but well worth the investment considering how crucial a role the Internet played in communicating his message in a controlled way. Consider this: While past candidates had to rely on the news media to give them coverage, Obama could release media announcements on his own terms, uninterrupted. He could also immediately rebut any false claims made by his opponents and quickly squelch any misleading statements.

Obama's campaign team was able to release announcements via YouTube, blogs, social networking sites, and other new media channels in an uninterrupted and completely strategic way. According to an August 2008 article an WashingtonPost.com by Jose Antonio Vargas, Obama's team "shot more than 2,000 hours' worth of footage and uploaded about 1,110 videos on Obama's YouTube channel — more than four times what was available on (his opponent) Senator John McCain's channel." By October 2008, Obama's YouTube channel had more than 100,000 subscribers (McCain's channel had less than 25,000) and videos were viewed more than 20 million times by the November 2008 election. In addition to the deliberate videos strategically released by the Obama campaign team, there were just as many videos created by his supporters. One of the most popular videos released involved the "Obama Girl," and her now famous "I've got a crush on Obama" video. The video showed an attractive girl, singing a light-hearted, comical song about her crush on presidential hopeful Barack Obama.

With more than 11.5 million views by election day, Obama Girl quickly became a recognized online superhero, being interviewed on top television news shows like Glenn Beck, Fox News, and MSNBC. Obama Girl was even awarded the "2008 Hottest Girl on the Net" by E!.

Aside from the comical, light-hearted videos, powerful images created by Obama supporters also emerged, such as the online music videos created by Black Eyed Peas' will.i.am. One of the videos was based on Obama's famous "Yes We Can" speech while the "We are the Ones" video featured famous faces like Jessica Alba talking about why they support Obama. Together, the videos have been viewed more than 15 million times. In addition to viral videos on YouTube, the Obama campaign team also leveraged the power and intimacy of mobile marketing by alerting supporters via text message of important announcements. In fact, they even announced his vice presidential pick by sending a text message to supporters' cell phones before announcing it to traditional media channels. Many questioned this tactic, saying that traditional media proposed a bigger venue for such an important announcement. But when you look back at Obama's entire new media strategy, it made perfect sense. Text messaging, like the strategies he used on the social websites, provoked one-to-one communication with voters. It gave voters an easy way to forward that message to friends at the exact time when it mattered most (like the text message he sent minutes before his speech at the Democratic National Convention, to remind supporters to tune in). Text messaging created a highly personalized feeling with the candidate, as well as a real time communication channel — which was beneficial on Election Day in reminding supporters to get out and vote. (See Chapter 4 for more strategies on how you can use mobile marketing for your business.)

The idea of the social web (also referred to as Web 2.0) is that success is based on two-way communication. You can't just put a message out there on a Web 2.0 platform and be done. In the example of Obama and his text messaging strategy, he had to have staff and volunteers take time to reply to the text messages that came back from supporters after each announcement. For example, supporters would text questions back inquiring about where their polling place was. Obama's team took the time to find the answers and text back.

A primary goal of new media outreach should be to lead consumers back to your website. This is the place you want your customers to take action, whether it is to purchase your product, set an appointment, or in Obama's case, donate funds to the campaign. According to a TIME magazine article by Karen Tumulty, "more than $10 million of Obama's second quarter contributions were made online, and 90 percent of them were in increments of $100 or less."

Obama's new media campaign team literally covered the social web, resulting in more than 5.5 million unique visitors to BarackObama.com by election time. That's 72 percent of the total traffic between McCain and Obama's websites. The traffic poured in through multiple new media channels such as social networking groups and profiles on Eons, MySpace, Facebook, LinkedIn, announcements on YouTube, blogs, and targeted microsites, even ads within online video games specifically targeting players in battleground states — all with consistent fonts, logos, and messaging. By election time, he had more than 3 million fans on his Facebook fan page. This did not even include all the fan sites set up by the public, outside his campaign team. He had more than 833,000 friends on MySpace, opposed to McCain's 217,000, 113,000 Twitter followers, opposed to McCain's 4,650, and according to Yahoo! Site Explorer, more than 2 million incoming links to BarackObama.com, while McCain had less than half as many link-backs.

Obama was not the first politician to use the Internet to propel his campaign. However, he was the most strategic and successful. In the previous election, we saw the Internet play a role in the rise and fall of presidential hopeful Howard Dean. He was one of the first to launch a successful grassroots online fundraising campaign with overwhelming success. However in the same way his grassroots campaign went viral, the "Dean Scream" led to his downfall, as it was watched over and over online, and even parodied in such YouTube videos as those created by Jib Jab.

The best thing about the Internet is that it provides a medium for all people, regardless of credentials or budget, to express their opinions and make a statement — and actually influence people in a dramatic way. However, in the same way a new media campaign can catapult your company or brand to record-breaking sales, it also opens you up to the social web, meaning consumers are talking, and their voices are heard.

Who is Using Social Networking Sites?

What television did for Kennedy in the presidential debates against Nixon back in 1960, the social web did for the Obama campaign in 2008. The social web is now officially mainstream, and a highly effective tool for reaching millions of people on a personal and engaging level. According to a poll by Forrester Research, 75 percent of Internet users participate in some form of social media, up from 56 percent just a year earlier (October 2008). While the growth of blogging has slowed a bit (grew only 10 percent from 2007 to 2008), starting a social networking profile grew 39 percent! Another sign that the social web has gone mainstream is that fact that, according to Forrester Research, the age gap is closing, and more people between the ages of 35–45 are getting involved in the conversation.

Determining the Right Social Networking Approach for Your Business

In this chapter we'll take a closer look at some of the top social networking sites and explore how real businesses are using them to leverage their brands, communicate with consumers, and sell more products. We'll explore sites like Facebook, MySpace, LinkedIn, YouTube, and Twitter as well as the new media strategies behind leveraging blogs. With so many options available, it's easy to get a bit overwhelmed.

In order to help determine the right social networking approach for you business, I interviewed several business owners and interactive agency executives to get their input on what is working best for them and their clients. Jimmy Hendricks, CEO of CollarFree.com explained that "The hardest thing [about launching a social networking campaign] is knowing what is right for your business. Each business is different. My best advice is to talk to other companies in your space that are not direct competitors and ask for advice. This saved us a lot of time and money." He went on to tell me that when choosing a social network on which to promote their t-shirt company, he recommended finding a niche site. Although they do have profiles set up on larger sites like Facebook and MySpace, they have found the most success with niche sites like FabSugar.com. "There is a community for almost every industry and 100,000 people in your industry is better than 10 million uninterested people," Hendricks said.

Daniel Khabie, CEO of San Diego based interactive agency Digitaria, agrees that finding the right social networking channel is key to promoting your business most efficiently on the social web. "Smart businesses are pushing their content onto niche sites like Sphinn.com (geared for online marketers), or even starting their own communities through services like Ning.com," explained Khabie. He went on to say that "Products get trickier, but Ziipa.com is an increasingly popular place for promoting your website or product for free. BzzAgent.com, a word-of-mouth community, is a great spot for asking community members to give their honest opinion on your product or service."

Too many companies try to reach out to the big social networking sites like Facebook or MySpace because that is where the most traffic is. However this may not be the place where consumers want to start a dialogue with you or hear about your products. Take time to find the social networking sites that are most popular with your target audience and make sense for your product or brand. As Jesse Pickard, Social Media Specialist for Razorfish summed up, "Know who you are trying to engage and pick the social networks that are most popular with your target. In short, fish where the fish are."

One way to find some of those niche sites is searching social networking websites on Wikipedia. The site shows hundreds of social networking sites by topic and registered users: http://en.wikipedia.org/wiki/List_of_social_networking_websites.

Engaging the Consumer, Not Selling

In addition to finding the right audience, equally important is how you get your message to them. Social networking sites are not a place for hard sales. They are a place to share ideas and communicate in a personal way. Thembisa S. Mshaka, author and founder of SEEIT Live, Inc., explains that, "As long as the company meets the networkers with respect without a heavy handed agenda to sell and sell only, I think all companies can benefit [from marketing on social websites]. But they must recognize the line of abuse and be careful not to cross it."

Companies need to offer content that is valuable and or entertaining to networkers. In November 2008, I worked with Sephora to help promote their web 2.0 holiday e-card called "Mistletoe Makeover." In less than one month, the site attracted more than 50,000 unique visits with an average stay of a little over five minutes. That's highly engaging! The only formal promotion of the Mistletoe Makeover we did involved sending the e-card and web links to key contacts in the media, including beauty blogs where our target audience was likely to be. It was posted on Sephora's Facebook page as well as emailed out to their millions of email subscribers. Why is Mistletoe Makeover a good example of a social media campaign? Because it truly engages the consumer, provides benefit,and entertains — it isn't just there to sell.

Here's how it works. Women visit the Mistletoe Makeover website and upload a photo of themselves. Using TAAZ.com virtual makeover technology, they can then choose from four different holiday makeup looks. After the look is complete, they can forward their new look to a friend with a wink or a kiss as an e-card. In return, you get a free-gift-with-purchase promotional code and can view all the cosmetic products used in your holiday makeover. As I write this, Mistletoe Makeover traffic is continuing to increase, as more women are creating makeovers and forwarding those looks to friends and family with holiday wishes.

Leveraging the Influence of Blogs

For CollarFree.com, online blogging efforts have proven most successful and the best return on investment. "We have built relationships with key industry bloggers in our space and now have the ability to launch new PR quickly," explained Hendricks. "This specific part of our marketing campaign grew traffic [to our site] by almost 900 percent in 90 days."

For TAAZ.com, I pack the Beauty Central blog with hair and makeup tips specifically written to attract new users via the search engines. The blog is responsible for directing thousands of new visitors to the primary site TAAZ.com every month. Every few weeks, I use a program like WordTracker.com to determine the top-searched keyword phrases, whether it be about Britney Spears' new hairstyle at the Video Music Awards over the weekend, or getting ideas for a great Halloween costume. I then forward these top-searched keyword phrases to the beauty blogger, who crafts stories around the topic. This helps ensure that when someone is searching for related makeup or hair ideas, TAAZ.com will come up. (See Chapter 8 for more details on how we specifically optimized the content on our blog.)

Lifecasting is a new term that describes the thousands of bloggers out there posting videos, pictures, and stories about their daily lives. Marketers are quickly discovering that certain high traffic bloggers can help promote their product in a genuine and personal way to their loyal readers. Skip down to the "Brand Ambassadors" section of this chapter for more on lifecasting and using existing networkers to promote your product.

Promoting Your Company through Facebook

With more than 130 million active users, spending 2.6 billion minutes on the site each day, Facebook is one of the largest social networking sites. It started as a social networking site for college students, but but today more than half of Facebook users are beyond college, with users over 25 years old accounting for the fastest growing demographic group. According to eMarketer (October 2008) and based on the August 2008 study by Internet Retailer and Vovici, Facebook is the social media site of choice for many US online retailers. "Nearly one-third of responding businesses said they had a Facebook page, compared with 27 percent that had a MySpace Page and just over one-quarter that had a page on YouTube." Similarly, a September 2008 study by Rosetta found that of the "top 100 online retailers in the US, 59 had a fan page on Facebook, up from 30 in May 2008. Among the 20 who added Facebook pages since that time were Best Buy, Toys "R" Us, Kohl's, and Wal-Mart."

Choosing between a Facebook Profile, Fan Page, or Group

Before setting up a Facebook Page, it is important to note the distinction of the different types of Pages. Making the wrong choice can result in your account and all the friends that you worked so hard to connect with disappearing! This was learned the hard way, after setting up the original TAAZ.com Facebook account as a user profile, rather than a group or a Fan Page, as it should have been.

Facebook groups and Facebook Fan Pages are both free, and intended for companies and organizations to use, while Profile Pages are designed for individuals. The Facebook group is a Page that enables Facebook users to join and share common interests. Facebook groups include local clubs, universities, sports teams, political or religious beliefs, or any other topic, belief, or hobby that people can share together. Anyone can start a Facebook Group Page, and send "bulk invites" to other users. This makes it a good choice for viral or event-oriented marketing, as well as hosting active discussions or getting quick feedback.

Facebook Fan Pages, on the other hand, are very similar to the personal Profile Page set up by individuals, but can be used by companies. The Fan Pages are visible to anyone, not just Facebook users and therefore are indexed by the search engines. (Note: Search engines can't view content that is behind password protected pages.) Facebook Fan Pages also have access to visitor statistics (Page Insights), which is valuable to marketers in understanding the traffic they are getting to their Facebook Page.

Buying Social Ads on Facebook

CollarFree.com used Facebook's targeted banner ads to drive quality traffic to their clothing site. "We had great success with their targeted ad platform when we were selling political t-shirts. You can hyper-segment their demographic really well and this helps ensure that you message the right people relevant information," explained Henricks.

Through its social ads, Facebook makes it very easy for advertisers to quickly set up a pay-per-click or pay-per-impression banner campaign targeting users with specific demographics. For example, you can select the users you want to target by location, gender, age, college, even by hobby, or specific keywords found in their profile.

When TAAZ.com first launched, Facebook ads were set up and cost around $0.45 per click (about half the price of Google Adwords for the same keyword phrases, and more highly targeted to our intended demographic). The ad featured a picture of attractive women and I varied the call to action, to test which produced a higher response rate. In November 2008 Facebook announced more upgrades to their social advertising metrics including a "Responder Demographics" report that allowed marketers to not only view click-throughs, but find out who specifically was interacting with ads in terms of age, gender, and geographic location. The "Responder Profiles" report allowed marketers to go beyond the basic demographics and see the psychographic information of these same users. This data is aggregated from user profiles and displays common interests such as favorite TV shows, movies, books, and music of the user who clicked on the ad.

Finding and Managing Your Friends on Facebook

The whole purpose of a Facebook page is to have friends. As a company, you want to have as many friends that fit your target audience as possible. One way to find friends, or alert your target audience about your Facebook group or fan Page is to post comments and join similar fan Pages and groups where your target audience is likely to be.

As a Tech Trends blogger for the *San Diego Reader* website, my job was not only to post articles on the latest Internet trends, but to make sure people found those articles and therefore ended up at the San Diego Reader website to see everything else the site had to offer. One way I promote my Tech Trends blog is by "sharing the link" with my Facebook friends on my profile page. However, I would also seek out new friends by posting the link on related group pages. For example, when I posted an article about how the Obama campaign was winning the race through new-media strategies, I looked to Facebook group pages for some like-minded followers. I came across an anti-Sarah Palin Facebook group, joined, and posted my link there. The move gained me some new friends including Thembisa S. Mshaka, author and founder of SEEIT Live, Inc. Mshaka is an avid Facebook user and uses it as an integral piece of promotional efforts for herself and her company. Rather than simply using Facebook to push a product, she uses her contacts to garner feedback about her projects. She even groups her friends into different categories, so that she can easily send messages to those that are most interested. "My core circle of influence resides here online and the exponential friending [through Facebook] has been consistent for me. I am organizing my friends into groups for targeted messaging," explained Mshaka. "Further, I have created groups related to my book that are flourishing. They serve as incubators for me to gather insights from people who care about me or my work. I poll the groups on everything from which author photos they like best to what kinds of terms I should look for in an endorsement deal. They also give me feedback on marketing strategy and execution. Additionally, it is amazing for making global connections that are signification and lasting; like twenty-first century pen pals that stay in touch." (**Note:** In order to group your friends into categories, click on the "Friends" tab and look under the "Friends List" area for "Make a New List.")

As a company, applications, quizzes, and other interactive widgets are good ways to get your company name out in a viral way among the Facebook audience. For example, the interns at TAAZ.com easily created and promoted a Facebook quiz titled "What kind of TAAZIE are you?" The quiz let users answer a series of questions about their beauty and makeup routine to discover which celebrity was most like them. They could then post the results of their quiz on their profile page, as well as forward it to more friends.

A quiz like this is a simple, quick application that anyone can set up via the tools available on Facebook. However, when companies take steps to develop something a bit more custom, the results can be exponential. "Digitaria created a Facebook application for Invisible

Children to help with the organization's Schools for Schools campaign, a competition among high schools to raise money for building schools in Uganda," explained Khabie. "Digitaria's Facebook application was integrated into Invisible Children's overall multi-channel marketing campaign, helping them reach Facebook's core student demographic. The Digitaria application enabled members to donate, as well as view compelling Invisible Children documentaries. By integrating Facebook into the campaign, Digitaria helped Invisible Children raise more than $675,000 to date; collect an estimated 37,000 donated books; and raise awareness by registering more than 2,000 schools in the Schools For Schools campaign."

Jesse Pickard, Social Media Specialist at Razorfish took a different approach. "We recently created a Facebook event engagement ad around the Victoria's Secret Fashion show. We reached over 122,000 attendees for the Facebook event by personally reaching out to organic Victoria's Secret groups on Facebook and targeting ads to Victoria's Secret enthusiasts. Success was measured by the number of RSVPs that we received for the event."

Six Easy Steps for Self-Promotion on Facebook

In addition to more company-centered Facebook groups and fan pages, many corporate executives and entrepreneurs are promoting their products and services by promoting themselves, personally, on social sites like Facebook. The formula for marketing yourself in today's digital world is to simply "make your business personal." In other words, the more you share your personal side with readers and "friends" the stronger they will feel about your work. With that said, here are six ways to promote your personal profile page.

1. **Update your Facebook page frequently**

   The more you update your Facebook page, the more reason it will give for your fans and friends to come back and visit. Each time you update your site, that information becomes available to all your friends via the News Feed feature. The News Feed feature even opens your information up to your friends' friends and is most successful at taking information viral. Stay away from posting mundane things like what you had for lunch, and instead post links, updates, and information that are all related to your brand and ideals.

2. **Upload photos**

   Photos help capture attention. Use colorful, casual, candid photos ... it will help your profile stand out more in the news feeds as well as communicate a human element through your work. If you specialize in one type of industry, it's a good idea to post photos of yourself that help promote that brand. For example, a music writer should post pictures of himself or herself with famous musicians or at a recent show.

3. **Use the blogging tools**

   "Notes" is Facebook's blogging feature. You can import your blog entries into the Notes function of your Facebook page. To do this, click "Edit Page." It will take you to "Edit My Applications." Select "Notes" then "Write a new note" in the upper-right. To import your blog entries from another site, follow the instructions from the Notes page.

4. **Use the discussion board**

   It will give you a direct way to communicate with fans, get ideas, and hear feedback.

5. **Post on walls**

   Use the "Post on the Wall" feature to reach out to potential new fans. When you post a comment on a friend's wall, all of their friends see it. This brings more attention to your profile and the potential to link up with more fans.

6. **Join groups**

   Joining specific Facebook groups opens you and your work up to more networks and potential fans. Post something on the wall of that group to get attention.

Getting Your Video Seen on YouTube

A 2008 Feed Company survey found that 71 percent of creative executives believe that viral video will be the standard marketing practice in one to three years. But with all the creativity out there, marketers are quickly learning that the hardest part about promotion via YouTube is getting your video to stand out from the clutter and be seen by the right audience.

One way to get your video found is through keyword optimization. When you post a video to YouTube, you get the chance to specify what category it belongs to, as well as include specific keywords. These should be the same keyword phrases for which you've been optimizing your website.

Another way to help get your video viewed is by posting it as a response to an already popular and related video. This way, people will see it as a link after they have viewed something similar.

Perhaps the easiest way to get your video seen on YouTube is to start a pay-per-click campaign through Google. Since the idea of buying keywords on YouTube is relatively new, there is little competition. An article from the *Los Angeles Times* found that even popular keywords such as "iPhone" were only around 10 cents per click, "a bargain compared with tens of thousands of dollars to place a video on YouTube's home page," (Guynn 2008).

Making Friends on MySpace

Since MySpace started as primarily a music interest site, record labels and musicians such as Madonna were quick to create profiles. Next came the entertainment industry, which has created profiles for movies such as *X-Men 3* and television shows such as *Family Guy* and *Kitchen Confidential*. Book publishers such as Random House are also leveraging the power of social networks by creating profiles for their authors and even for book characters (Rodgers, November 2005).

Check out the *X-Men 3* MySpace profile and you'll see a good example of how advertisers leveraged the power of social networking. The film's marketers have created an extensive profile on MySpace using all of the elements mentioned above, including allowing visitors a chance to enhance their own profile by expanding their visible friends network from 8 to 16 when they download a specific item. As of June 2006, the *X-Men 3* profile had captured more than 3,000,000 friends to help them promote the new movie (Kingdon, June 2006).

Some advertisers take steps to create a profile on MySpace, but keep things basic. For example, the Jack in the Box MySpace profile suggests that the company's marketing team knew it needed to participate, but wasn't quite sure how to leverage the space in an effective way yet. However, even a basic profile page such as this has generated more than 190,000 loyal friends who are actively posting comments about Jack and his food. When marketers from Jack in the Box are ready to leverage their profile power, either by requesting specific feedback on a new product or helping to promote a new menu item, much of the groundwork of finding their loyal audience online will already have been done. The important thing is that their marketing team created the pile and took the first steps toward entering the growing social networking arena.

As many major brands are quickly learning, moving too late into this area can actually hurt your brand. When a user sets up a profile on MySpace, they are give a URL, MySpace.com/Name, that they can customize. Anyone can pick a popular brand name as their MySpace name. It is against MySpace policy to sell or transfer user profile names. When Gatorade tried to create a MySpace profile, they quickly learned that their name was already taken. Gatorade has since had to use MySpace.com/GoFierce (after its new drink). The same is true with most major brands; just type in MySpace.com/yourbrand to see if someone is already using it. Top brands such as Pepsi, Ford, Mercedes, and many others are all being used by regular people, and currently there is nothing these companies can do to get their names back (Kingdon, June 2006). It is interesting to see how some users have literally branded themselves with the products whose names they have used. Depending on the person who is using these companies' brand names, this can be a negative or a positive thing.

When used correctly, social networks like MySpace can literally allow a person or brand to become an overnight success. The self-made celebrity Tila Tequila is a perfect example of this. With more than a million friends on MySpace and 30 million page views in one month, her success with social networking and with building exposure one-friend-at-a-time led to a feature on the magazine cover of *Stuff*, a spot on the entertainment news show *Extra*, and more. According to her MySpace profile, she is now endorsing products such as Game Boy Advance, is being featured in video games for Xbox and Playstation, and was even voted "number one Internet celebrity" by *Fortune* magazine.

Pickard advises businesses to take note of MySpace's distinct demographic and culture when designing out your initiative and that despite its large volume of traffic and press, MySpace may not be right for your business. As Mshaka points out, "[MySpace] is rife with people looking for pleasure instead of business — which is better for musicians than executives in my view."

Getting down to Business on LinkedIn

If the MySpace user is online simply for pleasure, the LinkedIn user is there strictly for business networking. On LinkedIn, you won't find pictures of people's pets or family vacations, but you will find people's resumes and corporate profiles. According to the site, "LinkedIn is an online network of more than 30 million experienced professionals from around the world, representing 150 industries." As a LinkedIn user for several years now, I have found it a great way to connect with other professionals, share ideas, and find new contracts and jobs. "For personal promotion, LinkedIn is the best way to manage your personal brand," agreed Khabie.

LinkedIn is also an excellent way for human resource professionals to find new talent, as well as businesses to promote specific B2B services. Similar to Facebook's social ads (except much more expensive!), advertisers can buy targeted ads on LinkedIn, and target them based on a user's profile. Typically when I log into my LinkedIn profile page, I'll see advertisements for local search engine marketing conferences or other promotions related to my industry. Ads are targeted to me based on keywords pulled from my resume and information posted in my profile.

Pickard recommends that businesses "take a long look at their API and Sponsored Questions offerings. Both provide great opportunities for brands."

Brand Ambassadors

Building up many friends from a grassroots level like Tila Tequila, or starting a blog that generates millions of interested readers takes a lot of hard work, time, and a bit of good luck. Rather than building up one of these profiles or high traffic blogs themselves, many companies are turning to existing networkers who already speak to their target audience as an influencer, and hire that person to promote their brand.

Lifecasting is a new term that describes the thousands of bloggers out there posting videos, pictures, and stories about their daily lives. Some have gained Internet celebrity by doing so. Marketers are realizing that leveraging these lifecasters can help catapult their brand within highly targeted social networking groups. For example, Beauty Addicts is using a popular lifecaster (iJustine), who also promotes the iPhone and iPod. According to the press release on February 20, 2008, Beauty Addicts "breaks new ground in cosmetic marketing by announcing their partnership with popular video blogger Justine Ezarik, a.k.a. iJustine (www.ijustine.com). Justine is one of the hottest lifecasters in the new-media world, with videos that reach a daily audience of hundreds of thousands and that have brought in over 22 million viewers to date."

Not sure how to go about finding a brand ambassador? One way is to do a search on YouTube or other high profile sites for your types of products or hobbies your audience is likely to be interested in, and contact those people with the highest amount of viewership or friends. Another way is to contact a company like SheSpeaks.com or BrandAboutTown.com. These companies help pair brands with online influencers.

Zappos' CEO Tony Hsieh has developed perhaps the most effective and time-efficient way to penetrating the social web by hiring employees who truly fit his corporate culture and brand. Since your employees are most likely using social sites anyway, if you hire those who truly mirror your brand and fit your target audience, it's like having brand ambassadors at your fingertips.

"You can't control every touch point like you could 50 years ago," he told AdWeek in a December 2008 article. "The only way to do it is instead of trying to 'control the touch points' is to get the right people with the right attitude, build the right culture, and the rest will take care of itself." As a result, there are more than 450 Zappos employees using Twitter alone, each working as a type of brand ambassador.

Twitter

Twitter. People either love it or hate it. Tim Ferriss, author of *The 4-Hour Workweek* called Twitter "pointless email on steroids" while Problogger.net's Darren Rowse claims, "If you are still not Twittering, you're missing out on what amounts to a worldwide virtual chamber of commerce networking event that is at your fingertips 24/7."

Twitter is a free micro-blogging tool that allows users to send text-based posts of up to 140 characters in length (called Tweets) in real time. Dell has credited the tool to producing $1 million in revenue due to sales alert Tweets. People who are interested in Dell products subscribe to Dell's Twitter feed. In return, they receive messages when products are discounted.

Digitaria used Twitter during the 2007 California wildfires, when timely information to homeowners was crucial. Khabie explained the strategy behind television station KPBS' website's use of Twitter. "During the 2007 California wildfires, the KPBS site, along with most of the area-specific news sites, experienced a huge spike in traffic from users wanting the most up-to-date information possible. However, the sudden spike left many news sites slow and unusable. To remedy the situation, Digitaria recommended to KPBS that it offer fire updates through a Twitter feed. The feed was then displayed on a special landing page that temporarily replaced the KPBS front page. Visitors could follow Tweets about the wildfires via their mobile phone or on the web through the quick-loading interface. The initiative was a success, keeping thousands of San Diegans updated on the path and destruction of the fires."

Find out Who is Talking about You

The thing that scares marketers the most about social media marketing is that true social marketing puts control in the consumer's hands. But rather than shying away from new media practices all together, it's important to know that if negative feedback is going to happen, it's best to get yourself in the conversation.

"The best branded Twitter accounts actively search out the Tweets where their brand is being mentioned and respond to the Tweeter when appropriate," Pickard said. "Example: Comcast directly responded to Tweets that mentioned problems with Comcast's service and offered solutions on the spot."

Once you start actively promoting yourself or your company online via the social networking, you are opening the door to two-way communication. You want to keep on top of what people are saying about you and your work — negative and positive. This way you can address fan concerns or play-off of "hot topics" and ideas your fans may have.

An easy way to monitor where your stories and name are being picked up is by signing up for Google Alerts (www.google.com/alerts). Simply use your company name as the keyword item, and you will get daily to weekly emails each time Google finds your name appearing online. You never know where you might end up!

Final Notes on Social Marketing Optimization Strategies

Trying to cover all the new media opportunities at once can be overwhelming for any business. After all, for the Obama campaign to take on the social web it took about $8 million, a high level, full-time marketing staff, hundreds of volunteers, and a passionate public to help propel the messages even further.

"The best piece of advice I have, beyond first understanding your business strategy and goals, is to focus," advises Khabie, "Too many businesses attack social media with the theory that more is better — Facebook and MySpace pages, blogs, and Twitter feeds, etc. But social media is extremely time-consuming and unless you have the resources to support all those initiatives, it's better to focus on one thing and be really good at it, and then move on to the next."

We are still in the early stages of discovering what works best for different industries and companies on the social web. As the space evolves, we are continuing to see new ideas and best practices emerge. While in the past, Internet marketing has focused on reach, acquisition, and conversion, the social web is about engagement and getting involved in meaningful conversations with your audience in a transparent way. With that said, get creative, have fun, and start testing your ideas. Use social networking sites to share ideas, create value, get feedback, show your expertise, humor, personal side, and test, test, test until you find a formula that works to achieve your marketing goals.

References

Bernoff, Josh. 2008. The Growth of Social Technology Adoption. Forrester Research. October 20.

Brohan, Mark. 2008. Great Expectations. *Internet Retaile.* September 1

Guynn, Jessica. 2008. YouTube pitches a familiar ad format, *Los Angeles Times.* November 13.

Kingdon, Mark. 2006. Ad Networks. MySpace campaigns. *Clickz.* June 20.

Morrisey, Brian. 2008. Q&A: Zappos CEO Tony Hsieh. *AdWeek*. December 22.

Rodgers, Zachary. 2005. What MySpace Means for Marketers. *Clickz*. November 21.

Tumulty, Karen. 2008. Obama's Viral Marketing Campaign. *TIME Magazine*. July 5.

Vargas, Jose Antonio. 2008. Obama's Wide Web. *Washington Post*. August 19.

____. 2008. Retailers Get Social with Facebook. *eMarketer*. October 29.

____. 2008. Rosetta, September.

____. 2008. The Agency Perspective. Feed Company, October.

CHAPTER FOUR
WHY USING MOBILE MARKETING NOW IS IMPORTANT

A number of years ago, businesses in Japan and Europe mastered the art of enhancing their brand and selling services by delivering text messages through cell phone and wireless marketing. So what has taken the North American business world so long to catch on to this highly effective advertising medium?

Entering the Mobile Marketing Medium

I remember first sitting down with my friends at Soapbox Mobile in 2003 to discuss mobile advertising opportunities for my clients. The cell phone carriers were finally making it possible for US companies to use the medium in ways that businesses in other countries had already been doing for years. But the medium was new, marketing people lacked an understanding of how it worked, and the costs involved were unknown (outside the entertainment world) — all of which combined to make it a hard sell. Since then more and more businesses are starting to explore the benefits of mobile marketing and are generating some exciting results.

With more than 205 million mobile users in the United States alone, 75 percent of whom are able to accept mobile ads and 13 percent of whom use text messaging daily, this opens up a whole new advertising medium for US businesses. And as with any new medium, the first movers will gain the most response.

Mobile marketing allows advertisers to reach consumers in real time and when they are more likely to take action.

Although teens worldwide currently lead in using text messaging, the older generation is quickly catching up. In fact, a study by Verizon Wireless found that 87 percent of women between the ages of 30 to 40 understand the importance of text messaging for their personal and business communications and actually see it as a more appropriate way of delivering a message in certain situations. With more than 65 percent of Americans carrying mobile phones, and 100 million receiving or sending at least one text message per week, mobile messaging is truly becoming a means to reach all age groups. Now, more than ever, is the time for businesses of all sizes to implement a mobile marketing campaign.

Using SMS (short message service) via mobile phones or wireless devices takes the power of Internet marketing a step further by sending a targeted message to a consumer when he or she is more likely to take action — when they are "on the go" and not simply sitting in front of a computer. Whether you are encouraging a loyal customer to bring a friend to your local coffee shop for a complimentary cup of java or trying to spark a political rally, mobile and wireless devices offer you an open door to your target audience at moments when they are most likely to respond to your message.

Unlike other forms of traditional advertising, mobile marketing represents a marketing channel that remains uncluttered. Which is why for mobile marketing to work, there must be respect on the part of advertisers when delivering messages using this very personal device. When used appropriately, mobile marketing offers an excellent way for businesses to strengthen their brand, communicate with customers, and create an overall buzz about their products and services. However, despite all the impressive stats, businesses in the US have been slow to jump into this new medium.

Leaders in Mobile Marketing

Several years ago, Hollywood was one of the first industry movers in North America to embrace mobile marketing, sending messages to moviegoers about opening nights or free tickets.

In 2004, Universal Pictures launched an ambitious mobile marketing campaign to promote the release of *Legally Blonde 2*. The motion picture industry understands that the success of movies is based largely on word-of-mouth promotion and opening-weekend attendance; therefore, the more ways they can reach their audience in the least amount of time, the better. Combine that with the statistic that young women and teens are the most enthusiastic audience participating in this type of marketing promotion, and you have your target audience for this movie.

The *Legally Blonde 2* mobile campaign included a sweepstake, themed ringtones, movie updates, and even the opportunity to receive blonde jokes on your phone. Users simply signed up by either text messaging the short code "LB2" to "BLNDE," or they signed up at the movie's website (Morrissey, June 2003). (More on how to set up short codes at the end of this chapter.)

In addition to simply promoting movies and entertainment through mobile devices, companies such as Amp'd Mobile and Soapbox Mobile now make it possible for moviegoers to search for movie times and locations and then purchase tickets directly from their phones. The MoneyClip™ application, which is created by Soapbox Mobile, enables Amp'd Mobile users to securely register their credit cards with their Amp'd Mobile number. Once registration is complete, subscribers can easily purchase tickets using a personal identification number (PIN) and their Amp'd phone.

Along with the movie industry, the music industry is definitely leading the way in mobile marketing. According to research by AOL in conjunction with Associated Press and the Pew Research Center, 40 percent of those aged 18 to 29 are likely to drop their landline altogether and depend primarily on cell phones. Fifty-two percent of adults keep their cell phones turned on all day (Sherman, April 2006). This provides an excellent way to reach a large number of tech-savvy people of all ages.

Numerous case studies have shown that mobile marketing to younger audiences is cost-effective in the music industry. For example, the Backstreet Boys took advantage of SMS during their recent tour, allowing fans to send them text messages during concerts. The messages (after being filtered for any derogatory comments) were then featured on a big screen behind the band. In addition to making fans feel more connected to the band during concerts, this generated additional revenue for the band. Fans were charged $2.99 per text message or picture sent, generating more than $25,000 in sales during the first three weeks of the tour (Newcomb, August 2005).

Although most studies suggest that cell phone marketing is primarily for youth, I don't believe this will remain the primary target

Use text messaging to personally engage your audience in an event — and gain the privilege of marketing to them again in the future.

audience for long. U2 and Madonna both appeal to an older demographic, yet U2 used cell phone technology to promote its ONE campaign and Madonna has completely embraced the mobile medium by offering ringtones, wallpapers, and tour updates.

Mobile marketing and sporting events

Allowing fans to send text messages to a big screen has spread to major sporting events, including Los Angeles Angels baseball games. However, instead of charging fans, advertisers use this as a chance to promote their brand side by side with the messages. For the Los Angeles Angels promotion, Verizon Wireless was a co-sponsor, allowing users to text their messages at no charge.

In 2006, Mavericks Surf Ventures teamed up with Soapbox Mobile to launch the "It's On!" SMS campaign that gave fans real-time updates on the event, along with surf conditions. Using mobile marketing was the perfect choice for promoting an event that brings together the world's top big-wave surfers on just 24 hours' notice to take on the infamous Mavericks break, a surfing location in Northern California. Thanks to mobile marketing technology, thousands of fans got a text message alerting them that the contest was about to start, receiving notice at the same time as the competitors did. The campaign also included a live webcast and an online store, as well as community-based features on the website. To become a part of the whole experience, fans simply text messaged the word MAVS to the specified phone number on their mobile phone.

Other industries get on board

Although the music and entertainment industries have been using mobile marketing strategies most aggressively, other industries are jumping on board, from Reebok to the US Navy, which uses a form of mobile marketing in its recruitment efforts. However, I believe we will see the biggest jump in mobile marketing in the travel industry.

According to M:Metrics, the average adult mobile web user is between the ages of 18 to 44 (predominately between the ages of 25 to 34) and has a large disposable income, with 22 percent earning over $100,000 USD (Marriott, June 2006). That's an excellent target demographic for the travel industry, as well as the auto industry. (More about mobile marketing for specific industries in Chapter 6.)

Imagine being a hotel owner and giving guests the option of checking in via their cell phones. The Luxor in Las Vegas is already taking steps to try this new approach because its check-in lines can be so crowded during holiday weekends; automatic check-in can allow a customer to bypass the lines. Take this idea a step further and offer your customers the option of mobile alerts while they are in town. You can team up with local restaurants, nightclubs, and theaters to give your guests coupons for dinner, VIP passes to the front of the line at a popular nightclub, or notification that tickets are still available for a show that night. The consumer benefits from the added personal touch and customer service provided by the hotel. The hotel and its partners benefit by strengthening their brand as well as inspiring word-of-mouth marketing. Imagine your guest having dinner with friends when he gets a text message alerting him that he and two friends have VIP tickets to the most popular nightclub in town, compliments of your hotel. Chances are, he will immediately show everyone at the table his text message and explain how it is an added benefit to staying at your hotel.

Use mobile marketing to reward your best customers. Text message them coupons, VIP passes, and useful alerts.

The idea behind all of these campaigns is to help build brand loyalty. It's about offering your customers increased value for doing business with your company. Consumers like brand loyalty programs; in fact, 75 percent of all US households engage in some type of loyalty program. People like to do business with brands and companies that are familiar to them, so rewarding them for their repeat business is the logical step to keep them coming back (Marriott, April 2006b).

GIS and Mobile Marketing

In 2006 AOL enhanced its local search and mapping services for Geographic Information Systems (GIS)-enabled devices. This provides another excellent opportunity for local storefronts and advertisers. The customer simply clicks the "locate me" function to quickly find movie times (via Moviefone), city guides (CityGuide), and maps (MapQuest). The GIS component in the phone makes it easy for users to find local information based on their exact position at that moment. As more advertisers get comfortable with using mobile marketing as part of their overall new media strategy, we will see more location-based campaigns producing exciting results.

Mobile TV

Another growing trend to keep an eye on is the more than 2 million wireless users who subscribe to mobile TV. This makes up 1.4 percent of the wireless base, and the number is growing. What's more, users who subscribe to mobile TV on their phones pay an average of $40 more per month for their cell phone service, making a very attractive audience for those marketing to a higher income, tech-savvy audience. At the time of publication, services like MobiTV, which are used by Sprint, Cingular, and Verizon's V Cast, are the primary mobile TV services in the US.

Free Minutes for Mobile Ads

Another emerging trend to consider when planning your mobile marketing campaign is offering free cell phone minutes to customers opting to receive mobile ads.

Virgin Mobile USA launched the first program giving customers the opportunity to win free talk time in June 2006. Microsoft's Xbox 360, Diet Mountain Dew, and the American Legacy Foundation's anti-smoking "truth" campaign are lined up as the first sponsors. Here is how it works: Customers will have the option to boost their cell phone minutes by as much as 75 minutes, earning one minute of talk for every 30-second commercial they agree to view. The campaign goes a step further by requiring customers to take a short survey at the end of the commercial about the product advertised. It's a great way for advertisers to get feedback on their product or promotion before they run the same ad in a more expensive medium such as television.

Although exchanging free cell phone time for ads may seem like an easy way to put your product in front of an audience, keep in mind that as more and more advertisers jump into this, it will get more cluttered. And as the novelty of the medium wears off, fewer customers will be likely to opt in to such ads. Although there will always be people who want something for free, this may not be your company's target demographic. If you are trying to reach older, higher income professionals, for example, this group is more likely to pay higher cell phone rates with no ads than cheaper services that expose them to potential cell phone spam. If your customer can't afford cell phone minutes, can they afford your product?

Text-to-Win

Although I am an advocate of developing useful content and meaningful, brand-building information for consumers, I have to admit that simple enter-to-win campaigns are a very effective way to encourage user engagement. In fact, simple text-to-win or text-to-vote sweepstakes are easy ways for mobile users to start participating in mobile marketing campaigns.

The classic beer Guinness implemented a new media campaign combining radio, print, and live events, with the centerpiece involving mobile marketing technology. The campaign, Guinness Radio Happy Hour, included radio personalities asking trivia questions and giving listeners a chance to win instant prizes. Soapbox Mobile worked with Guinness to help them set up the custom-branded short code 1759 (the year in which the beer was first made), to which users would text their answers. Listeners were notified instantly whether or not they had the correct answer and won a prize.

Trivia promotions and games are excellent ways to get people involved with mobile marketing. When NetInformer provided an in-stadium mobile system to the Oakland A's, baseball fans used their cell phones to participate in trivia games featured on the Diamond Vision screen. Once fans opted in and began playing, they were sent a wireless coupon for a discounted ticket and were asked to participate in future promotions.

The special ticket offers were sent to participating fans a week before the next game. In order to redeem the tickets, people had to show their cell phone code to the Oakland A's box office, or simply log on to the ticket website and use the web code provided to them.

The campaign proved to be a great success, yielding increased ticket sales, return attendance, deeper fan loyalty, and the beginning of a valuable database of mobile subscribers to be used in future marketing efforts. On average approximately 1,000 fans per game (more than 80,000 throughout the entire season) participated in the campaign, 15 percent of whom redeemed their discounted ticket coupons and 25 percent of whom opted to receive more messages.

When it comes to new technology, simple campaigns are best. Easy text-to-win campaigns are a great way to entice new customers to participate.

Because a majority of people carry their cell phones with them at all times, mobile coupons have a better chance of being redeemed than other types of coupon offers. According to NetInformer (2006), the average response rate to a mobile coupon is 12 percent for ticket specials.

As with any text-to-win campaign, whether it is promoted on the radio or at a major sporting or music event where you have access to a big screen, it's a good idea to show that people are in fact winning. Posting the winners' names or photos on the big screen with a message such as "It's not too late to win …" will encourage more people to sign up for your contest and to realize that they really do a have a chance to win.

The key to mobile marketing is to promote brand interaction while creating an environment that users get excited about. In other words, encourage users to have fun with the technology. At the 2006 Billboard Mobile Entertainment Content, Commerce & Applications Conference (MECCA), Soapbox Mobile did just that when they set up a "Mobile Treasure Hunt." The game gave attendees a chance to win prizes as well as experience the power of mobile marketing firsthand. Here is how the Mobile Treasure Hunt worked: Trade show attendees who registered their mobile phone numbers via a website or directly through their mobile phones could then participate in this game, which consisted of a series of clues and questions directly related to the conference, its sponsors, and the mobile industry. Every hour throughout the one-day conference, participants received a new clue via SMS, leading them through the symposium, its exhibition spaces, and panel discussions — and hopefully to some answers. At the conclusion of the conference, winners and prizes were announced (Marriott, April 2006a).

Running a campaign such as this at a trade show attended by potential business prospects is an excellent idea. It not only puts your marketing message immediately in the hands of key prospects, but the viral potential of such a campaign is huge. On average 24 percent of text messages are forwarded to other mobile phone users, and during a close-knit industry event such as this, the numbers could be even higher.

Using Mobile Marketing to Boost Retail Sales

Throughout the world, major retailers have been finding great success using mobile marketing to deliver discount coupons to their loyal customers. PlusOne lists a number of mobile marketing case studies on its website, www.plusone.com.au. In Italy, Dunkin' Donuts reported a 9 percent increase in sales due to its mobile marketing campaign. Cell phone users near a Dunkin' Donuts outlet were able to text a message to the number posted on billboards and broadcast on the radio to receive an instant free coupon or special offer to redeem in the store.

In Australia, a McDonald's ran a similar promotion combining coupons with a radio station contest. Contestants were sent promotional coupons by SMS to be redeemed at the local McDonald's, with an option to hear about future coupons from the restaurant.

In 2005 in the US, Starburst candy ran a mobile marketing campaign hoping to communicate with its teen audience. Starburst included its unique short code (JUICY) in specially marked packages, encouraging users to use SMS to win prizes such as iPods and flat screen TVs. Contestants were notified instantly if they won a prize, adding more excitement. With more than 60 million entries, the Starburst contest was the largest short-code campaign for a consumer product in US history. The company reports that its website traffic continues to increase as a result of the campaign.

Retailers of all sizes can participate in mobile marketing campaigns such as the ones described above. If cost is an issue, it may be a good idea to team up with other businesses in your area. According to an article by Lora Kolodny in *Inc. Magazine*, the storefronts at the CambridgeSide Galleria mall decided to try mobile marketing when no other forms of advertising seemed to bring in shoppers. The marketing team for the 116-store shopping center collected the cell phone numbers of more than 2,000 shoppers over a six-month period. Customers then received 39 discount offers from 19 participating stores. Offers included everything from "20 percent off at the register" to "Free appetizer when you dine with a friend." Shoppers who received the text message simply showed their phone to the mall's information desk and received a paper coupon. Eighty percent of all the mobile coupons sent were converted and the participating shops all saw a jump in sales (Kolodny, July 2004).

Steps for Starting a Mobile Marketing Campaign

Ready to get started with your own mobile marketing campaign? Great! Here are some important steps to take to ensure a successful campaign:

1. **Clearly identify your marketing objectives**

   As with any marketing campaign, define what you hope to accomplish via mobile marketing. Are you looking to collect more customer data? Do you need a way to announce events as they are happening? Or perhaps you want to implement a mobile campaign for branding or to gain more word-of-mouth exposure. Whatever the reason, it must be clearly defined ahead of time. That way, you can determine what type of mobile campaign will work best. For example, ringtones may help with branding, while a simple text-to-win promotion will help with gathering more customer data.

2. **Develop a detailed flow plan**

   Next, it is important to outline how the campaign will work. What type of process will the user need to go through to participate? Will they sign up via your website, directly through their cell phone, or in some other way? How will prizes be redeemed? Will there be a coupon code delivered directly to their phone which they can redeem at your storefront, or will you force them to visit your website to print out a coupon? When running a contest, clearly define the rules and/or legalities before you start the campaign.

3. **Identify how you will promote the campaign**

   Map out exactly how you will promote the campaign, as well as how you plan to integrate it into any pre-existing marketing channels. For example, will you promote it via your company website or storefront? Or will you create new radio or television commercials to promote the campaign? Also, since mobile marketing messages are delivered in "real time," think about what time of day you plan to release the messages for the greatest impact and response rate. You may have to test multiple release times to determine which is most effective for your audience.

4. **Get a short code**

   A short code is a four-, five-, or six-digit code a text message can be sent to or delivered from. For example, Guinness used the short code 1795 in their mobile marketing campaign; the Mavericks surf contest used MAVS. You can go to www.usshortcodes.com to check what codes are available; however, you will need the help of an aggregator to actually use a short code. Aggregators provide messaging connections to all or some carriers. Contact a company such as Soapbox Mobile or an Internet marketing consultant to help you.

The cost of a random short code is $500 per month, while a customized vanity code (such as the ones for Guinness and Maverick) is $1,000 per month. There is a three-month minimum for all codes, along with various set-up fees. The whole process of getting a short code and having it approved by each carrier typically takes 4 to 12 weeks.

5. **Get your campaign approved**

Because your campaign must function with the help of a carrier or mobile phone network service provider such as Cingular, Verizon, Rogers, Fido, etc., you must get their approval to run the campaign through their network. Again, this is where a company such as Soapbox Mobile or a new media marketing consultant can help you to get the certification you need. Once submitted, it typically takes about 10 business days to get approved by the carriers.

6. **Test, measure, and refine your campaign**

After you launch the initial campaign, continue to test what works and modify it accordingly. Since mobile marketing happens in real time, you can quickly measure your response rate to different promotions. You can also use unique mobile keywords in your campaign to test different timing or the effectiveness of different media. For example, have the television audience text a different word than the radio audience to measure which one generates more interest. (Learn more about measuring the results of your new media campaigns in Chapter 10.)

Customer Respect in Mobile Marketing

When I first mentioned my idea of writing a book which included encouraging businesses to try cell phone marketing, many of my friends were disappointed in me. In fact, my girlfriend Jaynine, who is also a pilot for a major airline, was downright angry with me!

"I depend on my cell phone! I don't want to get spammed! You know I work crazy hours, and I use my cell phone as my alarm clock when I am traveling," she said.

Like most professionals who rely heavily on their phones for important communications, Jaynine was concerned that her cell phone would go the way of email marketing, only worse. She was concerned that "cell phone spam" would interfere with her job, and the constant beeping of incoming marketing messages would keep her awake during her precious downtime when she had a chance to sleep before her next shift.

Just as ending email marketing spam starts with you and me — the marketer — keeping mobile marketing a safe and uncluttered medium also starts with us. Respect customers' right to privacy by always obtaining approval before sending commercial messaging. Continue to provide unique value to your customers, making mobile marketing something that is exclusive and sought after, rather than an intrusion.

As with email marketing, take the time to build your own list, and only send consumers information they have specifically opted for. In addition, always give them a way of opting out, and honor that. Finally, remember that all mobile marketing programs must be in accordance with state, provincial, and federal laws. You can learn more about the legality of mobile marketing by contacting the Mobile Marketing Association (http://mmaglobal.com).

The Future of Mobile Marketing

With the October 2008 launch of GI, the first cell phone to be powered by Google's open-source Android software, marketers should expect more changes on the horizon with how consumers use their mobile devices. In fact, Google co-founder and President Sergey Brin announced at the end of the GI demo posted on YouTube that more applications for the phone are on the way and that Google will pay the public to develop the best tools. In the video he says, "The best applications are not here yet, that's because they are going to be developed by you and many other developers just like you … we've set aside 10 million dollars that we'd like to give away to the people who develop the best applications using Android." That opens the door for a lot more "friendly" competition in the mobile space!

Other industry players besides Apple and Google are developing their own applications for mobile. For example, Samsung's new camera phones offer a Scanbuy barcode-reading application that allows users to learn more about a product at the exact moment they are considering purchasing it. Here's how it works: Find a product in a store and take a photo of the barcode with your Samsung camera phone. The Scanbuy barcode reader will scan the product, then instantly provide up-to-date information on that product, like customer reviews. It will even provide you with a list of coupons available and a price list for that same product at competitors' stores!

Amazon released a similar application in December 2008 that allows shoppers to visit any brick and mortar store, take a photo of a product they like, and then add it to their Amazon.com shopping cart — usually at a discount. The application was designed for Apple's iPhone, and gives shoppers an easy way to get "one-click" shopping delivered directly to their homes. Kooba's mobile visual search offers a similar type of scanning technology, but with a different angle. Simply use your camera phone with the Kooba application, and you can take a photo of any movie poster to get instant reviews and local show times.

With all these great mobile innovations on the rise, does that mean marketers should spend time and energy finding ways to market their products on all of them? Not necessarily. In fact, according to the November 2008 issue of OMMA Magazine, despite all the innovation and choice Apple's iPhone put into consumer's hands over the past few years, it is actually not the best selling phone (Tascio, November 2008). In fact, the much humbler Motorola Razr cell phone commands 40 percent of the global market. The BlackBerry also outsells Apple with 13 percent of the global market share, while Apple reportedly earned only 5 percent. Although these smartphones seem to get all the press and media buzz, they accounted for only 19 percent of handset sales in the second quarter of 2008 — still an impressive amount for any new device, but not yet something that all consumers feel comfortable using or feel the need to own yet.

I contribute three primary factors to the slow growth of these mobile web applications.

1. **Insufficient awareness and education**

   There is a significant lack of marketing to creating awareness about new applications, how to use them, and where to get them. Consumers don't know mobile apps exist, and if they do, they have no idea how to make them work for their phone.

2. **Cost versus value**

   Most of us have seen the YouTube videos or heard the horror stories of college students who received their first phonebook-sized bill from AT&T after they purchased their new iPhone. This high use cost has deterred most consumers from trying the latest mobile apps or even using mobile web or TV. However, with the release of Google's Android software, we may finally see relief from high use-costs and a complete shift in how we are charged for mobile Web use. Because Google's Android software will work on any mobile phone, the applications are no longer tied to specific phone service provider. In the very near feature, consumers may be able to access the latest mobile apps, regardless of cell phone brand or carrier, leaving more room for competition and lower access rates.

3. **Content not truly created for the mobile user**

   Most consumers don't know why they would want mobile content. Perhaps they tried mobile web a few years ago when it first came out, and before companies created WAP sites or those easily viewable via mobile web. The experience of trying to view a regular website on your mobile device was awkward.

Today, more companies are developing content specifically for mobile. Cosmopolitan, a magazine primarily targeting single women, developed "Cosmo Fake Calls" as a fun mobile application that is both brand building and relevant to its target audience in the US. With "Cosmo Fake Calls" you no longer need to have one of your girlfriends rescue you from a bad date. Simply go to Cosmopolitan's mobile site, and you can quickly request a "Cosmo Fake Call" (for about $0.99) to give you a good excuse to end a bad first date!

For years marketers have been hearing that "this is the year for mobile marketing" and although it still may not be the year for every business, it is getting closer than ever. Things are happening very fast in the mobile marketing space and marketers need to keep on top of what is happening, so that when it makes most sense for your business to get in the mix, you'll be ready. The future of mobile is already taking a quick turn to more open source applications, fewer restrictions from carriers, more consumer-friendly products, and solutions that make sense for a wider range of budgets.

For the most up-to-date information in the mobile marketing industry, or for more specific details on how to advertise on a mobile platform, visit the Mobile Marketing Association website at http://mmaglobal.com.

References

Burns, Enid. 2006a. Consumers Unsure of Mobile Phone as Payment Device. *ClickZ*, May 4.

____. 2006b. Tracking Mobile TV Audiences. *ClickZ*, May 24.

eMarketer. 2006. Dancing to a New Mobile Beat, May 23.

____. 2006. China Goes Mobile, June 22.

Greenspan, Robin. 2003. Wireless Gaining Subscribers Worldwide. *Markets Wireless*, October 17.

Kolodny, Lora. 2004. 112 Million Handsets Can't Be Wrong. *Inc. Magazine*, July.

Lieb, Rebecca. 2006. The Year of Mobile Marketing: Always Next Year? *ClickZ*, August 26.

Marriott, Laura. 2006a. Can Mobile Promotions and Sweepstakes Change Consumer Behavior? *ClickZ,* April 6.

____. 2006b. Building Loyalty via Mobile Devices. *ClickZ,* April 20.

____. 2006. Measuring WAP Ad Campaign Success. *ClickZ,* June 1.

Mehta, Nihal. 2005. Rock Txtn' Roll. *iMediaConnection,* September 14.

Morrissey, Brian. 2003. Hollywood Leads Mobile-Marketing Charge. *ClickZ*, June 20.

NetInformer. 2006. Oakland Athletics Case Study: 'Text-2-win' Trivia Promotion.

Newcomb, Kevin. 2005. OMG BSB R GR8! *ClickZ*, August 16.

Plusone. n.d. How SMS Is Building Business. www.plusone.com/au/smsstudies.

Sherman, Chris. 2006. AOL Enhances Mobile Search, Announces Study Results. *ClickZ,* April 3.

Tascio, Liz. 2008. Industry Watch: Buy Cell and Hold. *OMMA Magazine,* November 1.

Vodafone. 2004. Case Study — Vodafone Sponsorship of Ferrari: Supported by WIN Text Console. February.

CHAPTER FIVE

USING NEW MEDIA TO ENHANCE CUSTOMER SERVICE, TRUST, AND BRAND LOYALTY

New media marketing strategies provide companies of all sizes an excellent opportunity to give customers the feeling of one-on-one interaction without the burden of hiring more sales and customer support staff. When used correctly, new media channels can provide interactive content to help you build loyal and long-term customers. While mobile marketing can be used to simply remind customers of timely offers, your website can become your company's most powerful customer support tool. The goal of all new media marketing is to effectively keep communication lines open, to regularly remind consumers of events, new products, and upcoming promotions that they would specifically be interested in. The more you communicate with your customers directly, the more trust and brand loyalty you will build. Being a trusted adviser in your area of expertise and letting customers know how you can help them succeed in their business or personal lives are the keys to entering into their lives and into their social networks.

Creating a Trusted, Branded Personality for Your Site

News anchor Katie Couric is an example of a personality who appears trustworthy, friendly, approachable, and credible — a perfect combination for successful branding. As a result, Katie Couric, along with other branded personalities such as Oprah and Dr. Phil, can demand millions for any product they endorse because they make audiences feel at ease.

Creating an approachable and trustworthy image will help customers feel at ease when they interact with your company online.

Take a look at national and local news. The stations put a tremendous amount of effort into making sure you get to know their anchors and reporters so they can become trusted resources for news and information. Most local anchors lend their faces or voices to charitable causes and other local events deliberately to build up their own brand worth and increase the trust and credibility for the news stations they represent. Creating a trustworthy, credible, and approachable online brand for your business is a key to customer loyalty and to successful new media marketing.

The banking and financial industries are perfect examples of success based on consumer trust. Since the early 1990s when banking and financial companies started promoting their services online, they've had to work hard to convince customers that using their online services is safe and secure. Most consumers, including myself, were slow to try online banking or stock trading via the Internet. Besides the perceived security risks, the fact that banks kept their "we're bigger than you" image made them seem cold and unapproachable to the average Internet user who was looking for reassurance before using the new online services (Aaronson, March 2006).

Since then, banking and financial companies have gotten much better about providing accessible customer service online and reaching out to their customers in a friendlier way. For example, Wells Fargo does an excellent job of making online banking a comfortable and nonintimidating experience through its excellent navigation and user-friendly help menu features. In addition, they send a monthly email newsletter with small business financial and tax tips, making me feel like they truly care about my business success.

Financial giant Charles Schwab launched a "Talk to Chuck" campaign to make the global investment and financial services company seem more approachable to its online consumers. Although you can't actually talk to Chuck himself, the website does give customers a feeling that the company is approachable. Along with the Talk to Chuck graphic, the first image you see is the "Email a representative" button, which makes you feel like you can have direct access to your own personal representative. In addition, they have an "Ask Carrie" feature, which is an advice column written by Carrie Schwab-Pomerantz (president of the Charles Schwab Foundation), as well as a forum to ask her questions directly (Aaronson, March 2006). These features promote a feeling of personal, direct access to the company, and help build brand loyalty and trust.

Building Loyalty through Expert Web Content

Rather than creating online personalities, successful retailers such as The Home Depot are positioning themselves as experts, and they are gaining customer loyalty through their extensive online content and how-to guides. The Home Depot website, www.homedepot.com, sells hundreds of products online but is organized in such a user-friendly way that it makes finding the right product as easy as shopping in one of its brick-and-mortar stores. In addition to excellent navigation, the website showcases bestsellers in each category and detailed information to help consumers make informative choices. You feel as if you have your own personal sales rep guiding you through the process (Aaronson, March 2006).

A user-friendly website with lots of opportunities for direct contact with your staff is one way to make customers feel more comfortable doing business with your company online.

The Home Depot website doesn't provide online personalities or promote direct online communications the way Charles Schwab does, but their extensive Know-How section helps to solidify Home Depot's brand as the experts in home improvement information and products. Take a look at their Know-How section and find all types of home improvement information, from how to patch holes to how to build your own deck. They even provide you with a rating of how hard each project is. Know-How guides not only give customers a reason to return to the site again and again as they tackle each new home improvement task, they also provide search engines that have indexed hundreds of keyword-friendly pages. (Read more about search engine optimization strategies in Chapter 8.) This helps Home Depot find even more new customers looking to get started on home renovation projects. Although I think this site would be even more effective if they offered an "ask the expert" or live chat area, providing an extensive Know-How section with useful content is the next best thing for building credibility, trust, and loyalty.

Generating Consumer Trust by Letting Others Do Your Talking

Some companies, such as Amazon.com, have built consumer trust and loyalty by having their customers develop website content for them. This is done in the form of customer reviews and ratings of products. The most successful shopping sites have followed this practice, offering a forum for customers to rate products and give one another advice. Like most Internet shoppers, I have come to depend on these reviews when making almost all of my online purchases. Reading through honest customer reviews feels almost like gaining information from a trusted friend. Allowing customers to provide true feedback about your products on your site allows you to build instant trust with shoppers.

If opening up your products to customer reviews makes you nervous, consider a 2006 Keller Fay Group study finding that 62 percent of word-of-mouth feedback is positive. Consumers want to justify their purchases as well as find others with similar experiences. The Internet provides a perfect medium for them to do so. But what if your company ends up receiving some of the 38 percent of customer feedback that is negative or just neutral? The fact is, consumer feedback about your product is going to happen, whether it's on your website or posted somewhere else in cyberspace. Therefore, it's best to keep some control over it, so you can provide solutions to problems and make unhappy customers happy again. (Learn more about controlling negative publicity online in Chapter 7.)

Offering Excellent Online Customer Support

Creating consumer trust and loyalty online doesn't always require developing recognizable online personalities or spending a lot of time developing how-to guides. Sometimes just providing excellent customer service is enough to help put customers at ease and generate more confidence in your product.

After my laptop got stolen in Mexico City, I searched the Internet to find the perfect new one. A search engine directed me to a site I had never heard of before, called Newegg.com. Like any online shopper, I am a bit skeptical of unfamiliar sites and look for signs that I can trust the site with my credit card information (especially for a large purchase such as a laptop computer). Along with customer reviews, About Us pages, and awards and rankings listed on the site, what really put me at ease and closed the sale was their "live chat" feature. Being able to chat instantly in real time with a knowledgeable and friendly expert made all the difference. It made me decide to purchase the new laptop that I am using right now to write this book.

I had the same experience when I shopped online for a nanny cam so I could return to work after my first son was born. Although I ended up hiring an excellent nanny (whom I trust dearly, so I never hooked up the device), at the time, finding a website with online sales help to answer all of my nervous questions was essential. Will this camera show me what's happening at my house while I am at work? Can I view it in real time from any computer? Is it difficult to install? All these questions were quickly answered through a chat session with an online sales rep, who sent me a link to the exact web cam that would do everything I thought I needed. Just because more consumers are shopping online, this doesn't mean they don't need sales help. Having a live chat feature is an excellent way to help you close a sale, as well as give you the opportunity to make an "upsell" (to persuade the customer to buy a more expensive item).

Invest in adding a live chat feature to your site. It will help you turn more browsers into buyers!

Consumers want to feel in control of the products and services they buy. Traditional media ads are often limited to 30-second spots or small, static print ads. Before making their purchasing decisions, today's consumers turn to the web to find more detailed information about products they see in an offline ad. In fact, more than 50 percent of people who respond to television ads that feature a 1-800 number check for the product online before making a purchase. Once they are online, the best way you can give them confidence in your company and products — and therefore help to close a sale — is by providing customers with all the tools they need to make an informed decision.

Staying in the Forefront of Consumers' Minds

If you have a product or service that consumers buy regularly, it is essential that your new media campaign features an effective way to provide relevant information on a consistent and useful basis — without overdoing it.

Since I was eight months pregnant when I wrote this chapter, one of the things that got my attention was the BabyCenter.com email newsletter I subscribed to. This company did an excellent job of sending me very targeted and useful information that I talked about with other pregnant moms. BabyCenter.com newsletters were effective not only because of their useful content, but because of the timing. For example, when I was in the first part of my pregnancy, the newsletters came once or twice per month. When I was near the end of my pregnancy, with every week representing a new milestone, the email newsletters came every week. A subject line might have been "My pregnancy this week — 37 weeks." The newsletter offered a short paragraph about the size of the baby and checklists for making sure the nursery was ready for the new arrival. There was a link encouraging me to chat with other women who were 37 weeks pregnant. Similar to the idea of customer reviews, being able to chat with other women going through similar life experiences helped me build overall trust in and loyalty to BabyCenter.com.

The newsletter also contained a very targeted list of products I should be buying at this stage of my pregnancy. In fact, BabyCenter.com does an excellent job of showing new moms what products they need during different stages of their pregnancy and during the first years of motherhood. There are personal customer reviews of each product posted by other new moms, making the website a fun shopping experience. And, similar to how Home Depot has established itself as a trusted expert in home improvement, BabyCenter.com has positioned itself as a hub of all pregnancy and baby-related information. Whether you are looking for an answer to a specific health question or simply looking for comradery and advice on surviving the first year of motherhood, BabyCenter.com provides a single resource for all of your needs.

What does this baby talk have to do with your company? Numerous studies have shown that placing your ad on an already trusted website helps create trust in your brand too. In other words, if you don't have the time or resources to build your own extensive content database, online personality, or social network, find a website that has a strong following by your target audience and partner up. As a regular user of BabyCenter.com, I trust the products that are advertised on their site because (whether it's true or not) I feel like they are personally endorsed by BabyCenter.com — which I trust. BabyCenter.com understands the power of having loyal members and shoppers, and therefore knows its value to advertisers. To become an advertiser on this website, you must invest a minimum $10,000 USD. iVillage.com, which has evolved using similar member loyalty strategies, has a minimum investment of $15,000 USD to reach their audience. Charging higher prices for advertising allows these companies to be more selective about who advertises on their sites, which helps create a more exclusive, safe environment for their loyal members. The result is a win-win situation for all parties involved.

Using Targeted, Brand-Building Ad Buys

Product placement is something the entertainment industry has been using for decades. Examples range from game shows such as *The Price Is Right,* which showcases common household products, to movies such as *The Italian Job,* which featured MINI Coopers and brought them into the mainstream in North America. Finding the right website to promote your product is another excellent way to build your brand and effectively create awareness about your product. However, like product placement in traditional media, with new media channels it's more effective to truly integrate your product than to simply place banner ads. Think about providing original content through a podcast or sponsoring co-branded contests.

Timing and targeted placement are the core issues when you are considering new media ad buys. Although the same is true in traditional media ad buys, it is possible to get even more targeted in the new media world. While 90 percent of traditional television and radio ads are seen as "interruptive marketing," the Internet provides advertisers with an opportunity to provide a marketing message to a very specific audience in a specific mind state ... whether they are chatting it up on a social networking site about the best local club to visit that night or researching a major health concern.

Savvy marketers know that a targeted ad placement on a site that receives limited traffic is more effective than an ad on a less specific site that may receive 100 times the visits but has a far lower "conversion rate" (the percentage of visitors who take a desired action). Even major brands that are used to trying to reach the most viewers are learning that drilling down and placing ads on more targeted pages within websites is proving much more effective in finding new customers, as well as in strengthening their overall brand. Therefore, no matter how large a client's budget is, I never recommend purchasing "Run of Site" (ROS) ads; rather, I advise drilling down and getting their marketing message onto a page that specifically talks about something that complements their product — and will be seen when consumers are actively looking for a solution to a problem. Gone are the early days of the Internet when companies boasted who had the most traffic. Companies now understand that the most important thing is the quality of traffic, not the quantity.

Don't buy "Run-of-Site" ads. Instead, drill down and purchase space on a specific page where your target audience is likely to be truly engaged.

Let's look at the pharmaceutical industry as an example. If a pharmaceutical company were trying to promote a new migraine medicine, effective new media marketing would be planting stories about common migraine triggers and symptoms along with information about how the new drug can help, within the targeted pages of popular health websites like WebMD. Alternatively, a banner ad could be placed next to an already published story on headaches and migraines, encouraging readers to sign up for more information on this topic and a free trial of the drug.

When my two-year-old was running a fever, I turned to BabyCenter.com to look up little Calvin's symptoms and decide if his temperature warranted a midnight trip to urgent care. I was directed to a page called "When your baby has a fever," which was sponsored by Braun ThermoScan. The web page contained excellent information, including "What is fever," "When to call the doctor," and "At-home treatments," as well as more advertorial sections such as "Measuring body temperature" and "About the Braun Thermo-Scan." There was also a "Buy now" link. At the bottom of each page was a "Forward to a friend" link and a "Free fever guide" download by Braun. This is an excellent example of well-placed advertising content that helps establish authority and credibility for a brand.

In summary, take advantage of the need of today's consumers to research before they buy, and put your product in their research path.

Making Your Marketing Message Matter to Your Audience

Traditionally, advertising and marketing messages have often interrupted what a consumer is watching, listening to, or doing. With the birth of new technologies that are putting consumers more and more in control, interruptive marketing is becoming less and less of an option.

The most obvious way to get consumers' attention and to keep them from hitting the fast-forward button or scrolling past your ad is to talk about something that is relevant or interesting to them. However, when you do this, it may be difficult to make your marketing message seem genuine. Customers aren't going to forward an infomercial or advertisement to a friend, but they will forward or talk about an interesting new idea or an entertaining concept.

So, how do you create relevant content that keeps users' attention and encourages word-of-mouth marketing? Think about who your customers are and how you can help them. For example, as the CEO of a full-service web design agency, I hear all kinds of stories about problems business owners are facing with their websites. I take that feedback and turn it into helpful advice. For example, we send email newsletters to our clients regarding how to increase online sales, or we post articles on business websites or in business publications about how to build an email marketing list. I am providing clients as well as potential new clients with information they need, while establishing myself and my company as an expert that can help them achieve their goals.

Creating Great Content That Keeps Consumers Coming Back

Internet users are looking for three main things: entertainment, information, and/or a sense of community. Provide at least one of these key ingredients and your website is on its way to attracting some loyal customers.

BabyCenter.com is a perfect example of a website that effectively combines all three of these key ingredients to make an enormously successful web presence. In fact, it took the success of its online formula and now publishes a BabyCenter.com print magazine that is delivered free to all its members. Each issue of the magazine is scheduled to come out at the exact time when new moms and moms-to-be are looking for the kind of information it contains. For example, when I was in my third trimester, I received the issue dedicated to articles and information relevant to women going through those final months of pregnancy. BabyCenter.com continues to send well-timed magazines as your child grows, too. For example, you can flip through the issue about four- to six-month-olds and find photos and stories from BabyCenter.com members about what they did to lose "baby weight" or how they got their four-month-old to sleep through the night. Again, they are not only providing information and entertainment, but also bringing in that important sense of community that makes their website so popular. The magazine also provides lots of incentives to drive you back to the website, which helps reinforce the BabyCenter.com brand as the expert and leader in anything baby-related.

When Deckers Outdoor wanted to increase online revenue for their Teva shoes, they did so by implementing a Teva-branded community. The site contained relevant content about kayaking, trail running, and other outdoor adventure sports that their target audience was likely to be interested in. In addition it included contests and other interactive elements that got customers excited about the brand. As a result, the Teva.com site enjoyed more return visitors. In addition, those returning visitors spent more money each time they shopped than any new visitor, showing that building brand loyalty pays off (Atchison, April 2006).

Autobytel.com is another website where content and interactive information creates an overall trusted resource — which turns into solid dollar signs for the company. Autobytel.com provides all the information car shoppers need about their favorite cars, from safety features to price quotes, insurance to financing warranties. It even takes visitors on a virtual tour inside the car — all without the sales pressure of a dealer.

Women are a huge target for this type of service because they despise the pressure of hard sales. Women like to be able to research and get the information they need fast, in a no-pressure environment.

And Autobytel's marketing doesn't stop with the final sale. Users can log onto the "My Garage" section and get important updates on recall information, real-time service reminders, repair cost estimates, and even do-it-yourself tips. Or they can join an online forum on topics ranging from "Hybrids" to "Car Repair."

Creating a website of truly valuable content not only gives your site credibility but positions your company as an industry expert in your customers' eyes.

Creating custom content

Great content doesn't just refer to enticing promotions, stories, or graphics. It refers to anything on your website that encourages positive communication, reaction, and interaction between you and your targeted audience while delivering important information about your product, company, service, or beliefs. Great content can include message boards, chat rooms, video clips, Flash movies, or anything else that makes your customer excited about your website and product. However, be sure your content is relevant and appeals to your target audience. For example, you don't want a disruptive musical promotion if your customer is likely an executive logging on from work. And you don't want a large video download if your customer is most likely on a home dial-up computer. Knowing your target audience (more about this in Chapter 6) is the key to generating the most results from your website content.

If you choose to take the new media marketing approach of offering a content-rich website to boost customer loyalty and trust — as Home Depot, BabyCenter.com, and Autobytel have done — the key is to develop original content. Using syndicated content or buying content from other sources will not help build your brand or position you as an expert in the field. Websites with custom content are seen as the experts in their field and create loyal customers because visitors feel they can't get the information anywhere else. This means you will need to hire an in-house copywriter or outsource this job to an agency that can help you keep your content relevant.

Custom web content, unlike syndicated content, helps position you as an expert in your industry.

References

Aaronson, Jack. 2006. Gaining Trust Online. *ClickZ*, March 10.

Atchison, Shane. 2006. Teva.com: An E-commerce and Branding Case Study. *ClickZ*, April 20.

Burns, Enid. 2006. CNET to Distribute Video-on-Demand on TV. *ClickZ*, April 17.

Carton, Sean. 2006. Converging TV and Online through the Mouse. *ClickZ*, April 17.

Cohen, Heidi. 2006. March Branding Madness. *ClickZ*, March 16.

eMarketer. 2006a. Web Now a Mass Medium?, June 14.

____. 2006b. Missing the Message on Word of Mouth, June 16.

Evans, Dave. 2006. Up-and-Coming E-Marketing Channels. *ClickZ*, March 15.

Kaye, Kate. 2006. TiVo Offers Subscriptions to Branded Content. *ClickZ*, May 9.

Kingdon, Mark. 2006. Ad Networks: MySpace Campaigns. *ClickZ*, June 20.

Lindstrom, Martin. 2006. The Story of Branding. *ClickZ*, April 25.

Newcomb, Kevin. 2006. Microsoft AdCenter Goes Live. *ClickZ*, May 4.

Parker, Pamela. 2006. The Revolution Is Being Televised. *ClickZ*, April 7.

Rodgers, Zachary. 2005. What MySpace Means for Marketers. *ClickZ*, November 21.

____. 2006. With JogaTV, Nike Pushes Soccer Videos to U.S. Fans. *ClickZ*, April 17.

____. 2006. Nike's iPod Play Has Strong Web and iTunes Presence. *ClickZ*, May 24.

____. 2006. Miller Lite Extends 'Man Laws' Campaign to Web. *ClickZ*, June 16.

Schafer, Ian. 2006. When It Comes to Video, Integrations Is Integral. *ClickZ*, June 16.

CHAPTER SIX

DEVELOPING NEW MEDIA CAMPAIGNS BY TARGET AUDIENCE AND INDUSTRY

The key to successfully integrating your offline marketing efforts into the new media world is to understand who your target audience is, what their expectations are, and where they are most likely to be online. In this chapter, I will address some general demographic groups such as women, teens, college students, and seniors and look at what some top industries are doing online (and the money they are spending) to attract their target audiences. Although you may not see your specific industry or audience type listed, by reviewing the best practices and what works for other industries, you can come up with something similar for your company.

Defining Your Target Audience

When clients come to me for advice about how to drive more customers to their website, the first thing I have them do is make a list of characteristics of their ideal customers.

You can figure out what type of customer you are trying to target by answering the following questions:

- What age group are you targeting?

- Is your audience primarily male or female?

- What is your target audience's average household income?

If you don't know who your target audience is, start asking! Offer coupons or incentives in exchange for demographic data.

- How computer literate are they?

- Will they be more likely to access your website from home or work?

- Are they likely to have a high-speed or dial-up Internet connection?

- What are their hobbies?

- What part of the country are they most likely to live in?

- Are they single or married?

- Do they have children?

- What is their education level?

Knowing some basic characteristics about your customers will help you determine the most effective marketing plan and what website content and design will appeal to them. This will dramatically increase your success in delivering a clear, innovative message to a highly targeted audience.

The number one advantage of marketing online is that the Internet allows you to reach extremely targeted audiences, more so than any other form of advertising. So, the more you know about your customers, the better your chances of a successful campaign. And if you don't know who your target audience is, start asking! Give away a product or coupon to encourage your customers to share their demographic information.

By tapping into those features that can attract specific audiences to a website, you will be able to capture their trust, attention, and loyalty.

What Women Look For on the Web

According to WomenTrend, a Washington consulting firm, 80 percent of all household purchases are made or influenced by women, and since the year 2000 more than 52 percent of online shoppers are women. Women account for more than 50 percent of all the stock ownership in the United States and control $7 trillion in consumer and business spending. The number of women who own their own business is on the rise, and they are now the primary purchasers of electronic equipment online (Wegert, May 2006a).

McDonald's realized the importance of capturing this major consumer group when they introduced their new salads. Now when you pull up to a McDonald's drive-thru, you are greeted with colorful pictures of healthy salads with grilled chicken, low-fat dressing, and bottled water, rather than the traditional milk shake and Big Mac. As of 2006, McDonald's has sold more than 300 million salads and learned that the total bill of the salad buyers was on average double that of the primarily male consumers who purchased the standard cheeseburger and fries (Wegert, May 2006a).

Other top brands that used to focus on men have changed their product lines and marketing strategies to reach the highly desirable female consumer. For example, Home Depot launched its EXPO Design Center, which focuses on softer home improvement aspects such as interior design to attract more women shoppers. There was a time when my husband couldn't drag me into a Home Depot store; now, since the launch of the EXPO Design Center, I enjoy shopping for paints, window treatments, and other home-improvement items because of the more appealing visual layout of the stores. Plus, while my husband will get the Home Depot promotional flyers highlighting specials on new industrial tools, I receive colorful magazines from the EXPO Design Center highlighting interior decorating ideas and tips. Given the very strong influence women have over household purchases, getting women interested in home improvement projects was an excellent marketing strategy for Home Depot.

Obviously not all women are the same and you can't group them into one stereotypical demographic group. For example, a middle-aged power businesswoman would visit different websites and use new media in different ways compared to a young, single college grad searching for her first job or apartment. However, there are some common trends confirmed by multiple studies about how women in general use the Internet.

Women of all ages primarily use the Internet to save time and money. They see the value in 24-hour availability and speed in comparing prices in the absence of sales pressure. Which could be a reason why car and financial sites are now thriving!

Women also enjoy a sense of community. There is a reason that community-centered sites such as BabyCenter.com and iVillage.com are so successful. These sites not only give women a sense of community and comfort, they also help women with everyday life problems.

If they had to choose between the Internet and television, today's teens say they would choose the Internet.

The number of women who visit education, health, and family sites is dramatically higher than the number of male visitors.

Getting to Know Generation Y

Generation Y includes 60 million people born between 1979 and 1994. This includes the children of the baby boomers, so can also be referred to as the "echo boomers." This generation includes college graduates to today's tweens, and having been exposed to the Internet from an early age, they are more computer savvy than any other generation. They are less trusting of corporate media, more likely to ask questions, more likely to share opinions online, and find word-of-mouth an essential part of information gathering. As children of high-speed Internet and 24-hour cable channels, this audience is also very impatient, and expects things to be done now.

In order to reach today's teens, a new media campaign is absolutely essential. According to *BusinessWeek*, "[The Internet] is the Gen Y medium of choice, just as network TV was for boomers. Television drives homogeneity, the Internet drives diversity" (Neuborne, February 1999). Teens find what to wear, what to buy, and what to listen to from two main sources: their peers and online. And today's teens aren't just surfing the net, they are multitaskers. BurstMedia calls them "uber-taskers," meaning they are "simultaneously using various consumer technologies and media types; and using these technologies as complements to one another — producing an effect often greater than if consumed alone."

According to a May 2006 BurstMedia study, more than 80 percent of US teens spend at least one hour per day online, with 37 percent spending three hours or more every day. About 40 percent of the teens surveyed said they are simultaneously doing homework, watching television, or talking on the phone with friends while using the Internet.

What are all these teens doing online every day? Roughly three out of five (61.4 percent) visit social networking sites, with more teen girls than boys joining the sites. Half of US teens are playing online games or downloading music (*eMarketer*, June 2006e).

Targeting Teens and Young Men through Online and Mobile Gaming

The online gaming industry is exploding worldwide. A June 2006 report from DFC Intelligence predicts that the worldwide online game market will grow from $3.4 billion in 2005 to a whopping $13 billion in 2011 (*eMarketer*, June 2006c). Think of online and mobile games as an opportunity for building brand awareness and an excellent place to market your products aimed mostly at teens and young men. To serve this demographic, a new type of marketing has emerged called "advergaming."

Advergaming promotes a product, brand, or service through a game. For example, CoverGirl allowed web visitors to download a mobile game Girls' Night Out Solitaire, which features brand and product placement throughout the game. When consumers entered a UPC code for LashExact Mascara, they received $2.00 off the $5.99 mobile game download price (Marriott, June 2006).

According to Mobiltec's 2006 global research project, teens actually expect to be marketed to on their phones. And with regards to gaming, teens say they anticipate and expect advertising, special offers, alerts about new games, and incentives to rate and share their games with friends (Marriott, June 2006).

Although teens are open to advertising through their mobile games, the other demographic who is responsible for the largest downloads of mobile games are males between 18 and 34. This demographic may not be as accepting of advergaming. However, the fact that Microsoft purchased the in-game advertising company Massive Inc. in May 2006 shows that whether consumers like it or not, marketing on this channel will happen (Macklin, June 2006). Fortunately some studies have already been done to determine just how offensive advergaming is to older gamers. A study by Parks Associates in June 2006 revealed 38 percent of this demographic is willing to put up with advergaming if there is a chance to win prizes. The 18- to 34-year-old males surveyed also said that the least intrusive approach to advertising to them during a game would be product placement, followed by pre-game ads (Macklin, June 2006).

Reaching College Students through Online Social Networks

What started as an online hobby for some Harvard students, Facebook has quickly become one of the latest social network phenomena. Although the site attracts college students nationwide, Facebook is not set up like a massive social network such as MySpace. Rather, it is a network of many real-world communities. People log in and create groups based on real-life counterparts such as sororities and fraternities, political clubs, or athletic teams. Because each Facebook community consists of groups of people that often actually know each other, there is a higher level of respect and less likelihood of pornography and other offensive postings such as those you will see on MySpace. This makes advertisers more comfortable in associating their brands with the Facebook site.

In addition to creating online communities based on real world clubs and organizations, many people create communities based on favorite bands, hobbies, or other groups they want to associate themselves with. Facebook allows advertisers to associate their brands with these groups or to create a branded group of their own which students can join. Those who sign up for a branded group receive promotional emails and a brand logo on their personal profile. They can also join the branded message board (Newcomb, August 2005).

Matt Cohler, vice president of corporate development for Facebook, told *ClickZ*'s Kevin Newcomb, "I frankly didn't expect people would want to use the boards, but they do. Every day, there are women on the Victoria's Secret board talking about which products are most comfortable" (August 2005).

Video game developer Electronic Arts typically advertises on other gaming sites, sports sites, or other websites targeted to men, but it has found success in using social networking sites to reach its college-aged audience. Since word of mouth is especially important in gaming communities, Electronic Arts buys a new branded area with each new game it launches.

According to *ClickZ*, Facebook is among the top 10 highest traffic sites in the United States, with more than 65 percent of college students using it regularly. Such statistics confirm that such social networking sites are the key to reaching college-aged consumers, who are increasingly looking outside of traditional media and for more ways to control the information (and marketing messages) they receive (June 2006).

Finding Generation X

Generation X consists of 40 million consumers born between 1965 and 1978. Most are heavily into their careers and have started families. Because women and men in this generation keep their careers moving on the fast track, even while juggling family life, outsourcing personal and domestic tasks has become essential. According to MKTG Instructor's Edition, "Xers spend 78 percent more than average on personal services, more than any other group, and therefore spend 15 percent less than average on housekeeping supplies."

Because Generation X is one of the smaller demographic groups, most marketers seem to ignore them. The hesistance of most marketers of reaching out to this generation may also be because Gen X has a wider range of lifestyles, hobbies, beliefs, and income levels then other generations, and therefore are more difficult to pinpoint online.

However, when it comes to Internet usage, the Pew Internet & American Life Project (November 2008) estimated that 90 percent of Gen Xers use the Internet. That is only one percentage point difference than Generation Y. This means that if you are going to market to this group, do it online, and do it in the most efficient, straightforward way possible. Don't complicate the research or purchase step with anything too flashy or slow to download. Don't force them to join your social networking site or create an account to place an order. After all, with fast careers and new families, this audience is severely time-crunched! Generation X uses the Internet less for fun and more as a tool in efficiency. The Internet is an essential, time-saving part of their work day; they shop online for convenience, and use new media as a more efficient way to stay in touch with friends and family.

Internet Use by Seniors Is Changing Dramatically

While the current generation of adults 65 and older is still a bit skeptical about online shopping and using the Internet in general, over the next 10 years, as more and more baby boomers enter this demographic, we will see dramatic shifts in web usage. While seniors have traditionally been overlooked by marketers, especially in the online

When consumers enter a new life stage, such as parenthood or retirement, they are more likely to try new brands.

media world, today two-thirds of adults ages 50 to 64 use the Internet (compared to only 28 percent of those 65 and older) (*Senior-Journal.com*, May 2005). While today's seniors are still cautious online, and look for more basic websites without flashy technology or complicated downloads, the next generation of seniors is more likely to have broadband and will be used to using the Internet on a regular basis.

An estimated 33.2 million people between the ages of 50 and 64 are online in the US, which is more than triple the number of people 65+ who are online. In addition, the over-50 population is growing faster than the under-50, with 77 million baby boomers turning 60 in 2006. These soon-to-be seniors have an estimated spending power of $2 trillion, making them a very attractive new demographic for marketers to consider (*SeniorJournal.com*, May 2005).

As the baby boomers join the seniors demographic, they are expected to use the Internet to research and get help with major life issues such as investment planning, retirement planning, health care, downsizing of their home, and other topics related to the change in life stages. Placing your product or branded message in their research path is an excellent way to communicate with this audience. In fact, web pioneer Jeff Taylor, the founder of Monster.com, is so convinced that this demographic group will become more and more appealing to marketers that he spent $10 million to launch a new social network site specifically targeted at adults over the age of 50. The site, called Eons.com, modeled on MySpace, gives seniors a chance to create their own personal web spaces and communicate with others with similar interests. Taylor told the *Boston Globe* in April 2006 that he "scoffed at the traditional image of the retiree aimlessly puttering around the house until he dies." He went on to say, "I have way bigger plans for my life, and so does this whole generation."

Singles Have More Control of Their Time Spent Online

Singles are not online just to cruise the newest dating sites in an attempt to find true love. They are not constantly moving through life with the goal of getting married and starting a family. They are not sitting alone, in small apartments with small bank accounts, waiting for the phone to ring. In fact, singles are never really alone in the first place. They have roommates and co-workers and hundreds of friends on their favorite social networking site. They represent all ages, ethnicities, religions, and income levels — but the one thing that most of them do share is time. Control over their time and how they spend it. This means they may be more likely to spend time on social networking sites or take part in a promotional contest or game. However, if you do choose to target this audience, which by the way, makes up more than half the people in the United States (OMMA Magazine, November 2008), don't focus the promotion around stereotypes. Yes, even single people will buy luxury goods, cooking supplies, and vacations, so stop packaging these items around married couples and families.

Using "Life Stages" to Find New Customers

We've all gone through major events in life that move us from one demographic to the next. For example, the 16-year-old who passes her driving test; the high school senior preparing to leave home for the first time; the college graduate searching for his or her first job; the newly engaged couple looking to buy their first home; or the new parents searching for their first baby products. During these major shifts in life stages, consumers are most open to trying and accepting new brands, which makes putting your brand or product in their pathway critical for finding new, loyal customers.

People entering new life stages are also some of the primary contributors to CGM, or consumer-generated media. In other words, they are most likely to take part in, as well as be influenced by, customer reviews, blogs, message boards, and word-of-mouth promotion regarding new products and services. In fact, 90 percent of regular Internet users who are entering a new life stage actively research related information and 30 percent are likely to share negative or positive product or service information with other consumers. This is 20 percent higher than for the average Internet user (Blackshaw, September 2005).

The weight loss industry has been an advocate of CGM for years. When I worked with Jenny Craig International, real life success stories were the cornerstone to their online as well as offline advertising campaigns. New parents are also an excellent example of a consumer group that loves to actively talk about and post photos of their little ones online. Check out the major baby brand websites and you will see all types of community features. The best

ones will encourage parents to share photos and stories about their new babies. Catching new parents at this stage is critical, because once they have chosen a brand, it will most likely carry over if they have more children.

Think about the life stages that your target audience may go through, and then put your product in their pathway at the appropriate time. Offering a free sample or other incentive to get this audience to try your product at this crucial time is key. Combine that with customer reviews and testimonials they can trust, and you are on your way to building a long-term relationship with a new customer. Once they've considered giving your product a try, look for ways to get them talking about it in an honest way, to influence new customers. After all, chances are they are surrounding themselves with other people who are going through the same life stage.

New Media Technology Use by the Auto Industry

The auto industry is an example of an industry that can benefit from marketing to consumers entering new life stages. For example, think of all the life-changing events that precede the purchase of different types of cars, from family-style minivans to flashy sports cars.

Whether your target customers are going through a life passage or not, defining who exactly they are, and putting your product in their path, is key to a successful online marketing campaign. According to a 2006 "Audience Insite Measures" report from comScore Media Metrix, Internet users between the ages of 35 and 44 are 18 percent more likely than average online users to purchase an automobile this year. (In the US, this is more than 6 million consumers). When Internet users in this age group have two children, the report labels them as "established families" and says they are 27 percent more likely to purchase an auto in the next six months.

Similarly, Internet users aged 25 to 34 with one child, labeled as "new families," are 41 percent more likely than average Internet users to purchase a car in the next six months (*eMarketer*, June 2006h).

Although these two demographic groups may seem similar, according to the report, the sites these families visit online and their usage are actually quite distinct. For example, established families are visiting sites run by Disney Channel, Nickelodeon, Better Homes and Gardens, AOL Games, and MSN Games, while new families frequent BabyCenter.com, Orbitz.com, and more Yahoo!

branded web pages (*eMarketer*, June 2006h). Understanding which sites your customers are likely to frequent is important to promoting your brand message in the most efficient way.

In addition to well-placed ad buys on websites your audience is likely to visit, tapping into word-of-mouth marketing is huge for the auto industry. BMW is a perfect example of a company that zeroed in on its target audience and created an online promotion that attracted its ideal customers while also strengthening its overall brand and encouraging word-of-mouth marketing.

"We knew that 85 percent of the people who buy our cars are Web-savvy," BMW's marketing vice president, Jim McDowell, told *Business 2.0*. "Our buyers are fast-track people who usually have success early in their careers. They believe that the Internet is a wonderful thing" (Harrington, November 2002).

With this in mind, BMW launched an expensive film campaign. They enticed big-name directors (including Ang Lee, John Frankenheimer, and Guy Ritchie) and stars (including Forest Whitaker, Mickey Rourke, and Madonna) to create six- to eight-minute films that provided an elusive mix of entertainment and product showcasing. This was a brilliant way to ensure BMW kept its cutting-edge and high-end brand well positioned for its equally sophisticated and hip customers.

During the campaign, you could log onto BMWfilms.com and download Guy Ritchie's latest short film featuring Madonna in the backseat of the newest, coolest BMW being chauffeured at top speed through busy city streets. Or you could click over to an Ang Lee film, created soon after he completed *Crouching Tiger, Hidden Dragon,* and watch the bad guys chase a mysterious BMW driver (Clive Owen) who is escorting a young Tibetan llama to safety. (Note: The BMWfilms.com website is no longer live but you can find the movie clips on YouTube.)

Although BMW would not disclose the exact amount spent on the campaign, they did announce that if one million online viewers logged on, the campaign would be a success. They were thrilled to learn that well over three million visitors watched at least one film. And despite a cooling economy, BMW witnessed its highest car sales during the online campaign, exceeding the 40,000-vehicle mark.

Using new technology or doing something truly innovative online will almost always get attention. You don't need top directors

The average online consumer visits multiple sites before making a final purchase. Build a customer retention program to keep them loyal to your site.

and famous faces to make a campaign like BMW's films work for your small business or company. Just follow the same formula. For example, a really great Flash movie, photo, animation, or even an urban legend can start a buzz about your product or company. Think about the types of emails that get forwarded around the entire world: all those silly pictures, jokes, urban legends, and funny movie clips. Imagine incorporating a marketing message in such an email and watching your friends, family members, coworkers, and neighbors start forwarding the message to their email lists.

When Dodge wanted to promote its new Caliber model compact car to young, hip professionals, the company decided to allocate 20 percent of its advertising budget to new media marketing strategies to reach this technology-savvy group.

"We're trying to connect with young people, who are early adopters of technology. When you look at the youth group, you see their consumption patterns are online, in gaming, social networking, and video. We want to be where they are," Mark Spencer, senior manager of Dodge communications for the Chrysler Group told *ClickZ News* (Newcomb, March 2006).

In addition to adding technology such as an iPod-ready sound system to its new vehicles, Dodge is integrating branded messages with content on sites its target demographic is likely to visit. Along with running banner ads and videos on comedy, music, sports, and other special interest sites targeted to the 25- to 35-year-old demographic, Dodge is also talking about building a branded character on MySpace and working with PlayStation and Xbox to integrate the new car into four custom online games.

According to JD Power and Associates' 2005 New Auto Shopper Survey, 89 percent of online vehicle shoppers use a search engine during their buying process (Cobalt/Dealix, November 2005). This means that whether you are in charge of marketing a major automotive brand or are a local car dealer, maximizing your search engine marketing dollars is essential to getting some very cost-effective leads. According to Dealix Corporation, the cost of consumer acquisition when using search engine marketing tactics averages between $150 and $250 per vehicle sold, compared to traditional advertising methods, which average $550 per vehicle sold (November 2005). This shows that when done correctly, search engine marketing is not only a very trackable and measurable way to find new customers, but also much more cost-effective. (For more information on search engine marketing strategies and how to ensure a maximum return on investment on your pay-per-click dollars, see Chapter 7.)

New Media Marketing in the Travel Industry

With 83 percent of all US travelers using the Internet to research and/or book travel reservations, it is hard to remember just how we all planned our trips before the Internet. According to a May 2006 Consumer Preference Index (CPI) poll from Prospectiv, of the travelers who use the Internet to research or book their trips, 30 percent research but do not actually book online, while 31 percent research *and* book their trips through online travel sites, and 21 percent book travel arrangements directly through the website of the hotel or destination they will be visiting (*eMarketer,* June 2006f).

The CPI poll revealed that more than 88 percent of travelers who book their trips online would like to see more content and even more specific information about the destinations and accommodations they plan to book.

Although the online travel industry is highly competitive, with sites such as Travelocity, Orbitz, and Expedia spending millions on traditional as well as online advertising, the good news for new or smaller travel sites is that the typical online user still searches an average of three to four travel sites before making a final decision on where to book. For example, customers will use a site like Expedia to search for the best price, but still go to Southwest.com just to confirm they found the best deal before booking (Smith, June 2006). In order to keep consumer loyalty in this industry, it is essential to build customer retention programs such as points programs or other incentives to keep visitors coming back.

Another way to maintain customers' interest in your site and ensure repeat visits is to collect email addresses and send a regular email newsletter. The newsletter should not only include interesting content about featured destinations you are trying to promote, but should also incorporate time-sensitive promotions and special discounts for loyal users or those who refer friends. The more you can target the newsletter and promotions to specific customer interests, the better your response rate will be. Therefore, when requesting customers' email addresses, be sure to also ask them what types of

Eighty-eight percent of travelers who use the Internet to plan their trips say they want more information about the destinations they plan to visit.

promotions they would like to receive. For example, are they interested in weekend getaways? Cheap tickets to international destinations? Family-friendly trips? Adventure travel? The more you know about your audience and what interests them, the more you can target specific promotional campaigns — and the better results you will see in all of your marketing efforts.

According to a travel association industry survey, 38 percent of travelers who book online have an annual household income of more than $75,000, and 42 percent have graduated from college. These highly affluent, educated, and often middle-aged (between ages 35 and 54) clients are not necessarily price shoppers, and they are more technology savvy than the average Internet user (*eMarketer,* June 2006f).

If you're looking to target the higher income, more affluent traveler and you don't want to compete on price, you must offer some other incentive such as unique packages based on specific activities. Be sure to use email marketing to inform customers of new packages as well as additional ways your services are unique. Basing your packages around a specific date and activity is a great way to create an incentive for your loyal customers to book a trip they may not have thought about otherwise. For example, offer a "Girls' Getaway Weekend to Palm Springs Spa" or a "Father-Son Fishing Trip Package to Jackson Hole, Wyoming." Offering your customers trip ideas and incentives for minivacations throughout the year is a great way to encourage customer loyalty and set your site apart from other travel sites.

To distinguish itself, Orbitz is offering special features such as its new OrbitzTLC program. In addition to offering city podcasts about specific travel destinations, monthly events, and things to do, the most unique new feature is travel alerts that can be sent directly to your email, PDA, or cell phone as well as to clients, family members, or anyone else who should be notified of a delay in your flight schedule or change in gates. It's extra customer service features and fun with technology that help set the major travel sites apart from each other and encourage loyal customers who are looking for more than just price comparisons in a travel site.

Expedia, also a major player in the online travel industry, generates 36 percent of its traffic from pay-per-click search terms. They have found that the most effective search terms are map-related —

in other words, travel-related terms that mention a specific destination, for example, "Hotel in Cabo San Lucas" or "Cheap flight to San Diego." Expedia has also found that 39 percent of its traffic comes from other travel sites such as TripAdvisor.com, from which about 12 percent of Expedia's traffic comes. Finally, Expedia averages about 3 percent of its traffic from email marketing (Hopkins, April 2006).

Travelocity, on the other hand, which spent more than $40 million on traditional and online ads in 2002, is the first travel site to really experiment with some of the newest media marketing avenues. In 2006 it teamed up with travel guru Rick Steves, who is recognized from his popular television and radio shows, to create a branded travel podcast. It is also perfecting its pay-per-click keyword buys, and is reporting an average of 72 percent conversion rate.

TripAdvisor.com understands the need for more detailed travel information online, so it centered its 2006 campaign around 25 downloadable guidebooks for popular destinations such as Paris, New York, and Cabo San Lucas. Since the bulk of content on the TripAdvisor site is generated through consumer reviews, the guidebooks consist of information posted by users. To download the guide, users need to provide their email address, and when they do so, they can also enter a contest to win a trip. If they forward the link for the guidebooks to a friend, they are eligible for an even bigger trip prize. TripAdvisor plans to implement an email marketing campaign with the addresses it collects in this way.

In addition to promoting the guidebooks online, TripAdvisor is also promoting the new travel content through traditional advertising methods such as radio spots, print ads, and display ads where tourists are most likely to be, such as in San Francisco trolley cars. So far, the campaign has had enormous success, proving that useful content really is a great incentive to get the attention of online travel seekers. During the month of March alone, TripAdvisor attracted more than 20 million unique visitors, and as of June 2006 it reported more than 3.5 million registered members (Parker, June 2006b).

There is no doubt that we will see continued growth and therefore more competition in the online travel industry as more and more people look to the Internet as their sole resource in researching and booking travel. If you are in the travel industry, it is essential that you implement some of the following new media marketing strategies:

1. Set yourself apart from the competition by offering unique site features, new customer service technology, and/or special packages based on activities your customers are interested in.

2. Implement some guerrilla marketing tactics and make sure your website address is listed where online travelers will encounter it. Remember that as they research their trips they not only visit their favorite travel sites, but also frequent blogs, search for related articles, and seek out customer reviews.

3. Provide content on your website about specific destinations and things to do there, as this will increase the odds of reaching new customers via search engines and word-of-mouth marketing.

4. Have an experienced search engine optimization consultant optimize all of your content pages to ensure they are correctly indexed by search engines and can easily be found by prospective travelers.

5. Whether you are an already established or a new, smaller travel site, invest in some very targeted pay-per-click advertising. Because travel-related search terms are becoming more expensive by the day, I recommend using an experienced Internet marketing consultant or agency to help you set up and monitor the campaign to ensure your PPC dollars provide you with the best return on investment.

6. Once you get customers to your site, give them a reason to stay loyal by offering promotions and incentives to join your email newsletter and/or to tell friends about your services.

All of these elements are essential to reaching the online travel consumer.

Nonprofits and Charities: Building a Trustworthy Web Presence

While all types of companies will benefit from building a trustworthy and credible online presence, for the nonprofit industry this concept is the cornerstone to success in new media marketing efforts. While competitive industries in the travel and automotive sectors benefit from exploring the latest in new media marketing strategies, nonprofits and charities can keep things simpler. For these groups, the key is the website itself and how it makes the visitor feel. It is absolutely essential that a charity's website not only reflects the organization's values and goals but also portrays a credible and professional image that will encourage donors or volunteers to want to get involved with the organization.

Donors are becoming more and more accustomed to researching charities and nonprofit organizations before they donate or get involved. In fact, according to the Kintera/Luth Nonprofit Trend Report, 65 percent of donors visit the websites of charities they support, and 40 percent always go online before deciding to give. Yet so many nonprofit and charity sites do not have any call to action on their sites, and do not encourage users to take the actions the charity intends for them.

From 2003 to 2004, online donations increased more than 50 percent. On average, donors who contribute online tend to give more overall (over 50 percent more) than donors who do not contribute online. (You can request the complete report at www.kinterainc.com.) Therefore for nonprofits hoping to attract more donors, having a well-designed website is absolutely essential.

In addition to having a professional web company design your nonprofit site, implement the following steps to give your site a more trustworthy appearance and to encourage visitors to take the actions you have in mind:

1. Identify what exactly you want visitors to do when they find your site, whether it be to volunteer, donate money, or take another action. Once you have determined this, make sure that every page on your website encourages visitors to take this action. (This same rule applies to commercial sites as well, and is covered in more detail in Chapter 8.)

2. Whenever you are asking a user to provide payment information online, whether it is for a donation or to purchase an item, provide a physical address and phone number. Make this contact information clear, and even post it at the bottom of every page as well as in the "Contact us" section of the site. This is key to establishing trust.

Save time by using a paid service such as RegisterLocal.com, which allows you to create one master business profile and submit it to all local search services at once.

Dedicate at least 20 percent of your total marketing budget to new media strategies.

3. Target the colors, design, imagery, and tone of the website to those who would be most likely to get involved. Take some design risks and show your organization's personality. Make sure your site "talks" to your audience and gets them excited about your mission.

4. Treat your website visitors in a manner that is true to your organization's mission and values. If your organization supports people with visual impairment or elderly people, ensure that your website contains large, easy-to-read text and is ADA (American Disabilities Act) compliant overall.

5. Keep your website content current. If your home page still showcases a fund-raising event you did three years ago or lists press releases from last year under "What's New," people will be less likely to donate online and/or take your organization seriously. Outdated websites make users wary of getting involved and especially wary about providing payment information. An outdated website makes visitors wonder if the organization is still active, and if so, whether it has the personnel to carry out the group's mission.

6. Make information about donating or getting involved easy to find by including it in the primary navigation, as well as on every page of the site.

7. If your website is asking for online donations, provide very detailed information about where the money will go. Make donors feel safe about giving their money and inspire trust that it will be in good hands.

Local Marketing Strategies with Search Engines

Studies have shown that the overwhelming majority of online buying happens locally. The transaction may be made online, but the product or service is actually attained or originates from a nearby location. Typically, an online shopper will use a search engine and type in the specific product or service along with his or her city. This also signifies that he or she has sufficiently researched the product or service and is now close to making a final buying decision. Therefore ensuring that your local business shows up on the search engines when a consumer is ready to buy is essential.

In addition to general search results, Google and Yahoo! will list some local sites at the top of the search (based on the location of your computer's IP address). We are in the middle of seeing many changes in search results on all major search engines, as they offer both general and local results at the same time. There are also many local websites being developed, where you can access a database of local businesses.

As with the local search technology itself, a majority of the available listing options and ad buys are also still in a beta-testing phase. A "city" and "service" search one day on Yahoo! or MSN can provide completely different results a week later. For example, today some top search engines may showcase local ads for Verizon SuperPages and Yellow Pages (localized search engines), where tomorrow they may be offer their own pay-per-click listings. And some search engines only sell ads in *pay-per-call* format, whereby your ad displays a unique 1-800 phone number, which forwards to your business number. (You only pay when someone calls this assigned 1-800 number.) There are other search engines that force you to pay a monthly fee for a minisite listing, and only then is it directly linked to your actual site. Some local sites make you bid for the highest listing while others use a first-come, first-served listing basis.

At the time of writing, the local search market is in constant flux. My advice for getting your company listed on local search engines is to hire an expert to help you keep up with all the changing trends in the local search market. And hire that someone to help you now! Getting on local searches is likely to get more expensive and more competitive as more businesses realize the importance of these targeted searches, and as more consumers get used to using the local search features on their favorite sites.

When New Media Marketing Is a Must

I cannot cover all industries and every possible target audience, but most industries do share common problems, and what works for one industry often works for another. Therefore reviewing the best practices and successful marketing strategies of other industries is helpful in determining how your own company can find success online.

As we have explored in this chapter, some organizations can succeed with merely having a well-designed website while others absolutely must incorporate more advanced new media marketing strategies to maintain a foothold in a competitive marketplace. For industries where people spend a significant amount of time researching before they buy, such as automotive, real estate, and computer equipment and services, it is essential to make your website the center point of your campaign and to dedicate at least 20 percent of your overall marketing budget to new media marketing strategies. If, however, you have a well-known and widely available consumer product such as a soft drink, candy, or other grocery store item, your brand can most likely survive without a heavy web tie-in. However, I still recommend trying some online marketing strategies, as even these industries are seeing some important results from new initiatives. (Read about the Starburst candy mobile marketing example in Chapter 4 or the Pepsi/Britney Spears case study mentioned in Chapter 7 and outlined in my book *Low-Budget Online Marketing for Small Business,* also published by Self-Counsel Press.)

Even if you don't have a product that lends itself to being directly sold online, keep reading. The next chapter is all about controlling your brand image and public relations through Internet marketing, which is important for any company.

References

Aaronson, Jack. 2006. Learning From Different Industries' Best Practices. *ClickZ*, June 30.

Blackshaw, Pete. 2005. CGM: The Parenting Megaphone. *ClickZ*, September 20.

____. 2006a. Do You Know How to Find the Marketing 'Ex-Spot'? *ClickZ*, May 2.

____. 2006b. Word of Mouth Begins with Consumer Affairs. *ClickZ*, May 16.

Cobalt/Dealix Search Marketing Team. 2005. Search Engine Marketing for Dealers. *Dealix Dealer Newsletter*, November.

eMarketer. 2006a. Online Travel Slowdown. June 6.

____. 2006b. Catching up with Commuters and Pedestrians. June 8.

____. 2006c. Online Gaming Draws Global Competition. June 12

____. 2006d. Parents Love and Hate the Internet. June 13.

____. 2006e. The Net: Teens "Gotta Have It." June 15.

____. 2006f. Have Mouse, Will Travel. June 16.

____. 2006g. The Internet: Where the Money Is. June 20.

____. 2006h. Car Talk Online. June 30.

Harrington, Ann. 2002. Take 2: Why Is BMW Back in the Movie Business?

Business 2.0, November 1.

Hopkins, Heather. 2006. Expedia Online Marketing Success. *Hitwise.com*, April 13.

Kaye, Kate. 2006. New Nonprofit Launches Multi-Million Dollar Cross Media Campaign. *ClickZ*, May 5.

Lamb, Charles W., Joseph F. Hair, and Carl McDaniel. 2008. *MKTG Instructor's Edition*. Thompson Southwestern.

Lieb, Rebecca. 2006. Where's Your Social Life Headed? *ClickZ*, June 30.

Macklin, Ben. 2006. In-Game Ads to Grow; Targeting the 18-34-Year-Old Male. *eMarketer,* June 20.

Marriott, Laura. 2006. Advergaming: Next on the Mobile Marketing List? *ClickZ*, June 29.

Neuborne, Ellen. 1999. Generation Y. *BusinessWeek*, February 15.

Newcomb, Kevin. 2005. Facebook to Offer New Ad Options. *ClickZ*, August 15.

____. 2006. Dodge Looks Online to Reach Young Buyers. *ClickZ*, March 31.

____. 2006a. BMW Uses TiVo Technology to Improve Product Placement. *ClickZ*, June 21.

____. 2006b. Interpublic Teams with Facebook. *ClickZ*, June 29.

Parker, Pamela. 2006a. Billion-Dollar Brands' Word-of-Mouth Ambitions. *ClickZ*, June 23.

____. 2006b. TripAdvisor Promotes Itself as Web Surfers' Destination. *ClickZ*, June 30.

Retirementhousingonline.com. 2006. 50+ Internet Usage Statistics and Research.

Saunders, Christopher. 2006. Travelocity Drops $40 Million for New Ads. *ClickZ*, May 28.

Seniorjournal.com. 2005. Strong Internet Use by Tomorrow's Seniors Means Big Changes for Market. May 19.

Smith, Brian. 2006. New Players in Travel Search. *ClickZ*, June 27.

Sostre, Pedro. 2006. From Maui, With Love: A Comprehensive but Dated Hawaiian Travel Site Gets a Modern Makeover. *Revenue*, May/June.

Stelter, Phil. 2006. A Local Search Roundup. *ClickZ*, May 25.

____. 2006. Social Media as Local Search Guides. *ClickZ*, June 22.

Sterling, Greg. 2006. A Real Estate Vertical Search Roundup, Part 1 and

Part 2. *ClickZ*, June.

Thomases, Hollis. 2006. What Agencies Need to Know About Local. *ClickZ*, May 23.

Wegert, Tessa. 2006a. Marketing to Women: More Than a Media Buy. *ClickZ*, May 18.

_____. 2006b. The New Baby Boom. *ClickZ*, May 25.

Woolford, Leah. 2006. Top 10 Travel Forecasts for 2006. *Usdm.net*.

CHAPTER SEVEN

CONTROLLING YOUR BRAND IMAGE AND PUBLIC RELATIONS THROUGH INTERNET MARKETING

"Management is lying to us to avoid the bad press for the company, and do not care about our safety," writes a Wal-Mart employee on a blog site entitled WalmartSucks.org.

"I think walmart is the devil because its trying to take over the whole world with stores that has stuff in them made by children slaves … " writes another blogger.

The very nature of the Internet lends itself to people freely sharing ideas, and the ease of doing so in today's new media world leaves all companies (and people, too, for that matter) susceptible to consumer-generated media (CGM). With the ease of forwarding an email, uploading a comment, or sending a text message, consumer feedback in today's media world can be absolutely viral. In order to help to control what is being said about your company or products, it is essential to not only understand the reach and technology involved in the creation of CGM but to actually take part in it. Regain some control over what is being said about your company by jumping into the world of CGM through blogs, content optimized for search engines, and well-thought-out online PR strategies.

With all the negative CGM about Wal-Mart online, including a site called WakeUpWalMart.com which boasts more then 180,000 supporters, Wal-Mart hired a PR agency to help combat the negative press. One of the key components of the campaign was to enlist

One way to combat negative press is to better optimize the positive press, so that is appears higher on the search engines.

"guest bloggers" to write positive things about the company, with corporate headquarters feeding positive news stories for the bloggers to post online.

Ideally, starting up your own marketing campaign to encourage positive feedback about your product should help your brand gain some control over what is being said about it online by essentially working to dilute any negative press. The more positive pages you can produce (and strategically place) about your company, the more likely the positive news shows up on the popular search engines ahead of the negative press.

Positive CGM about your company can be extremely powerful in strengthening your brand image. However, in the same way positive consumer feedback can help your company online, you have to be ready for the negative feedback that often comes with it. In today's new media world, business owners have to develop a thick skin because the Internet provides an open venue for anyone to post critiques about your company, products, service, brand, or even employees.

When Chevy decided to hold an online contest to promote its new Tahoe SUV, it didn't exactly encourage an outpouring of love for the Chevy brand. Instead, the contest became the platform for anti-SUV groups, anti-war-in-Iraq comments, blogs against global warming, and pro-environment blogs, all bashing the Chevy Tahoe SUV. Although you won't find these satirical ads on television or Chevrolet.com, they still linger on the Internet even though the contest has ended. You can still find a few of the negative spin-off ads posted on high-traffic sites such as CNET.com and YouTube. Many of the ads start off sounding like a legitimate Chevy Tahoe commercial, but then slice in comments like "Nobody is walking … they are seeing the world from the window of their SUVs." A similar ad says, "We had ice caps. They melted. The water dried up. Last time you voted Republican. This time vote Democrat."

In a time of skyrocketing gas prices, growing concern about global warming, and the ongoing war in Iraq (which many believe to be about oil), the Chevy Tahoe caught the brunt of the political and environmental backlash against America's "need" to drive SUVs. So although Chevy was on the right track when it created an Internet marketing campaign centered on CGM, in this case opening the communication lines with the public about its product severely backfired because they simply chose the wrong product to feature. Perhaps if the contest had featured a hybrid car or another model that gets better gas mileage than the Tahoe, the campaign may have turned out very differently.

When Converse, a footwear company, created a similar ad campaign, their results were more positive. The ad campaign allowed consumers to create their own 24-second video promotion with a chance to win $10,000. The campaign drew more than 250 entries in the first three weeks and more than 3 million unique visitors to the site during the first few months. This example shows that using consumer-generated media as the centerpiece of your Internet marketing strategy can be extremely effective — particularly if you are promoting an uncontroversial product such as tennis shoes (Stein, April 2006).

The Benefits of Online Press Releases

Creating a forum for CGM and encouraging positive word of mouth are all part of implementing a successful online PR strategy. However, a traditional press release is also an important piece of the new media mix — for several reasons. The first reason is obviously to attract media attention. With more than 92 percent of today's journalists turning to the Internet to research stories, making sure your latest press release is easily available online and in the right place at the right time is key to getting journalists' attention (Crowell, June 2004). There are now services such as PRWeb.com that allow PR professionals to submit company press releases to targeted media lists as well as to top news portals and search engines such as Google News.

Another important reason for making press releases available online is that it increases your company's search engine ranking. However, in order to make this happen, I recommend having a professional search engine optimization (SEO) consultant take a look at your press release to ensure that it is optimized for keywords, products, and services. Additionally, if search engine optimization is your primary goal for implementing an online PR campaign, have the consultant help you write the press release from the beginning, focusing on the keyword phrases with which you want your site to be found. Assuming your press release is optimized and correctly posted on your website, online press releases help your overall search engine ranking in the following ways:

1. *The more content you have on your site, the more keywords search engines will find.* Be sure your press releases are written in a way that promotes the key products and services that you want search engines to find.

2. *Some search engines will rank one site higher than another if it has newer, more relevant content.* Including links and dates to new press releases on your home page will alert Google that your site has new content and is more up to date than a competitor's site that may still have links posted from last year.

3. *Top search engines such as Google also look at link popularity to determine how high to rank a website.* Link popularity is determined by how many other websites link to yours, thus showing Google how important your website is to the industry. The more credible the site that links to you, the more that link weighs. So, for example, getting your press release or a news mention on a major site such as MSN or NYTimes.com will give you a much higher link popularity score than 10 links from your friends' personal home pages.

Creating buzz around your press release

In order to gain the benefits of increased search engine ranking and media exposure from your online press release, you'll want to make sure that people actually are interested in your story topic. Below are some tips for increasing your chances of creating buzz around your press release and maximizing the potential benefits that come with a successful online PR strategy.

1. **Play off what is already being talked about**

   Whenever you can tie your press release into an upcoming holiday or a hot news story or a topic that the media is already covering, you have a better chance of getting attention.

2. **Be a little controversial**

   You don't want to be so controversial that your PR efforts backfire, but creating a press release about something that makes people want to talk is a great way to increase the shelf life of your press release. Being controversial doesn't mean sparking a major controversy. Sometimes it can just mean becoming the first company in your industry to implement a new technology. Another idea that always sparks media interest is reporting interesting survey findings. For example, when Dove released its Dove Global Study and reported "only 2 percent of women find themselves beautiful," they received a lot of media attention and buzz on the Internet. Referring users to a blog at the end of your press release to learn more and share thoughts on the topic is another great way to open the communication lines and get consumers talking. Getting consumers talking about your topic is an excellent way to show journalists firsthand that this really is something that their readers may care about as well.

3. **Be the expert**

   Whenever you release a press release that showcases your authority on a topic, this helps position you and your company as the industry expert. As more media professionals get used to seeing your company name or the name of a person within your organization as the expert on related-industry topics, the more likely they will be to call you for interviews and quote you in stories. Creating press releases that help establish you or your company as the expert in your industry will have long-term benefits.

4. **Get to know journalists in your industry**

   Become familiar with the regular writers who contribute articles to magazines, websites, or other media outlets where your target audience is likely to be. Then send those journalists ideas that are related to the articles they write. Everyone can use a little help coming up with new creative things to write about.

Optimizing your press release for RSS feeds

Another way to ensure that your press release reaches as many corners of the Internet as possible is through the use of RSS feeds. RSS (Really Simple Syndication, or Rich Site Summary) is a way of quickly syndicating content on the Internet. Originally RSS was primarily used by news websites to gather headlines and stories. However, it is now being used to syndicate all types of online content from blog postings to podcasts. RSS is no longer used only by journalists; now consumers have set up their own subscriptions to RSS feeds based on their hobbies or other topics of interest. Sources such as PRWeb.com allow you to create RSS feeds easily as part of submitting your press release.

However, just because you submit your press release through an RSS feed doesn't mean it will automatically attract media attention or consumer interest. With so much content flowing online these days, it's important to optimize your RSS feed, just as you would any other element of online marketing.

To help ensure your RSS feed gets picked up by the right sources, remember the following tips:

1. **Spark interest with an attention-grabbing title**

   Ensuring that your RSS title is interesting enough to stand out from the thousands of other titles is key. If no one is interested in your title, no one will bother to read on.

2. **Use keywords in your title and your feed description**

   Along with an attention-getting title for your feed, also use relevant keywords that will help search engines find your feeds.

3. **Show benefits to the consumer**

   An RSS title and feed description must show a clear benefit to the reader. In other words, your title and description should be focused on consumers and how your news topic will help or interest them, rather than be focused on your company and its accomplishments.

4. **Using the RSS feed image option to help strengthen your brand**

   Including your company logo in your news feed will not only make your title stand out more, it will also help to brand your company for specific RSS topics, helping to establish you as a leader in that industry. As more readers get familiar with your company brand and the type of feeds you provide, they will pay more attention to those feeds.

Your Brand, Your Trademark, and the Search Engines

In the online world, your brand strength is often tied directly to how consumers see your brand on the search engines. For example, when you type in your company name, does your corporate website show up, or does one of your affiliate's show up ahead of yours? Or perhaps you've just learned that your competitor has purchased the top position for the keyword phrase "your company name." Or worse yet, are the first few pages of Google's listings flooded with links to negative consumer blogs about your product — blogs over which you have no control?

According to a study released by Hitwise, 15 percent of searchers who type in a brand-name query end up on a competitor's website, which means taking control over your online brand image and online PR surrounding your company is more important than ever. The same study showed that 75 of the 100 most popular searches in February 2006 involved trademarked brand names, which means people are searching by company name, even if they don't end up going directly to that company's website.

One of the reasons consumers end up on a competitor's website is because of the pay-per-click options available that allow companies to use competitors' brand or product names to promote their own websites. Remember the advertisers discussed in Chapter 1 who profited off the companies who advertised during the Super Bowl by purchasing keywords that correlated with competitors' television ads?

Although more attention is getting paid to the unfair practice of buying keywords with the brand name of competitors, until any official laws on the matter are enforced, marketers have to look to the policies implemented by each search engine for guidelines. For example, Yahoo! only allows brand owners, resellers, comparison-shopping sites, and informational sites to bid on trademarked keywords. Google allows anyone to bid on a trademarked name but won't allow everyone to include the trademarked name in ad copy.

Find a partner who is already established in the new media space to help jumpstart your campaign.

Strengthening Your Online Brand through New Media Partnerships

A powerful way for traditional businesses to gain access into the new media world is by joining forces with an already established new media company.

When Pepsi launched its first major new media campaign in 2000, it partnered with Yahoo!. The partnership allowed Pepsi-Cola to gain immediate access to Yahoo!'s technology, as well as its growing online audience. The partnership went on to become the centerpiece of one of the most successful advertising campaigns in Pepsi's 106-year history.

The campaign drove consumers to the website PepsiStuff.com to redeem points earned by entering special codes found on more than 1.5 billion caps of plastic Pepsi bottles. Each code was worth 100 points, which could then be used to shop online for prizes such as clothing and CDs.

Taking the campaign online had definite advantages. Right from the start, Pepsi-Cola saved more than $10 million simply by not having to print prize catalogs. And through the partnership with Yahoo!, Pepsi-Cola didn't have to worry about the technical issues related to developing and managing the high-traffic e-commerce site where customers redeemed their prizes. In exchange for its technical assistance, Yahoo! received co-branding on all Pepsi Stuff bottles and in-store displays, as well as $5 million worth of advertising on television and in print.

During the online campaign, overall national sales of single portion Pepsi bottles jumped 5 percent. That is a huge accomplishment considering that overall soda sales increased by only 0.2 percent during the previous year. But more importantly, the online campaign allowed Pepsi to collect 3.5 million customer profiles, which included valuable demographic information such as names, email addresses, zip codes, and dates of birth. Once Pepsi's marketing team confirmed who their target audience was, they were able to create additional marketing campaigns that were extremely effective both on- and offline. In fact, the demographic information collected during the Pepsi Stuff campaign solidified Pepsi's decision to place Britney Spears in that year's Super Bowl commercial. The Britney Spears campaign proved to be a huge success with Pepsi's target audience. In only nine days, more than 1.1 million people logged onto Yahoo.com and downloaded the television commercial.

The 2000 Pepsi-Cola campaign exemplifies an extremely successful approach to combining traditional and new media marketing. The campaign allowed Pepsi to quickly extend its brand to online users through its partnership with Yahoo!, collect important customer data for future marketing efforts, and track customer actions and behaviors — as well as increase offline sales. The campaign was also one of the first to show how using the Internet as an alternative medium to post your television commercial dramatically increases its shelf life and the reach of that commercial.

Nike is another major corporation hoping to strengthen its brand through new media marketing. In 2006, Nike announced its plans to team up with Apple and iTunes to enhance its customer base and brand through the development of new media content as well as the creation of a new product. The new, co-branded product is a running shoe with a wireless iPod nano receiver, which allows runners to listen to their favorite iPod tunes while monitoring speed, distance, and calories burned. Runners can then sync the information to the online membership community to compare stats and compete in virtual races online.

The Apple/iTunes brand is enhanced by the celebrity athletes on the NikePlus.com site, such as Lance Armstrong, who use online video testimonials to discuss the importance of music in their workouts. In addition, Nike has developed branded content on the iTunes site through the "Nike Sport Music" section, which promises to feature music and podcasts to motivate runners.

Co-branding works when there is synergy

A co-branded campaign such as the one between Yahoo! and Pepsi-Cola and also between Nike and Apple/iTunes works best when both companies provide distinctly different services or products but share similar audiences. An example is the very successful marketing partnership between Sony PlayStation and Red Bull energy drink. Both appeal to teenage boys yet offer very different products.

The bottom line is that consumers actually like co-branding. It helps them to choose among the hundreds of brands out there. In fact, the American Marketing Association released a study that found that when appropriate, two brands pushing a product are

Consumers like co-branded campaigns. It helps them make a choice among the hundreds of brands available.

much better than one. In the study, 80 percent of those surveyed said they would buy a digital imaging product if it were co-branded by Sony and Kodak. However, only 20 percent said they would buy the same digital imaging product if it were made by only Sony or only Kodak.

In another study, published by the *Journal of Consumer Marketing*, the power of co-branding was confirmed in a taste test of potato chips and dips. In the first trial, researchers attached a well-known brand name to both the bag of chips and the carton of dip. In the second trial, they served the test group the exact same chips and dip, but used a fictional brand name. The researches also tested the reaction of name brand chips combined with a fictional brand dip and vice versa. The result? The participants rated the name brand chips and dip combination significantly higher than any other combination of brands. This study concluded that when high-quality brands team up together, it strengthens consumers' approval rating (Washburn, Till, and Priluck, December 2000). Furthermore, if an unknown brand teams up with an already established popular brand, the partnership, if done right, will not only help increase the unknown brand's sales, but also strengthen that brand. The study also found that if a popular brand teams up with an unknown brand, it will not hurt the popular brand (as long as that company keeps a close eye on the quality of the customer service and product of the less-known brand), but sales won't necessarily be increased either. The best bet for a strong brand is to team up with an equally strong partner.

However, like with chips and dip, co-branding partnerships must make sense. If it isn't completely obvious why two companies should partner up, then the benefit to the consumer won't be obvious either. For example, in 1998 AT&T formed an alliance with British Telecom and backed it with more than $10 billion, but it failed in less than two years. The reason? Consumers couldn't quite grasp the connection between the two megabrands.

The failure of AT&T's co-branding partnership with British Telecom shows that successful co-branding is not about how large your budget is, but rather how appropriate the synergy is between the two brands. Co-branding provides a perfect avenue for small businesses as well as large corporations because with the right partner, you can share marketing costs, technologies, and resources, and one well-thought-out campaign can strengthen your brand and give you access to a whole new customer base.

Co-branding guidelines

Before contacting a potential partner or planning your next co-branding campaign, consider the following questions:

1. What will the brand partnership convey about the customer? Will the partnership make the customer feel more educated? More classy? More hip?

2. What characteristics do the two brands and the consumer share? Are they both innovative? Cutting-edge? Dependable? Make sure that your new campaign image does not clash with the image of your current customer base. You never want to lose that current base, just build on it.

3. What benefit does the brand partnership provide to the customer? Does it save them time or money? Make the immediate benefit to the customer very clear in your campaign.

4. Is the partnership user-centered? Is your goal to provide the best solution to the customer? It should be.

5. Is there an equal value for both brands involved? The relationship must be equal or it won't work.

6. Is the value of the partnership easy for customers to understand?

7. Does the partnership open up your company to new customers? Will it help you upsell to your current customers?

Finally, remember that co-branded partnerships will only help your business if they complement your overall business goals and brand. Don't lose sight of what you are trying to accomplish online, whether it's online sales, credibility, or new clients. Make sure that all your content, promotions, and partnership activities encourage visitors to take the actions you intend for them to take.

New Branded Television Content

As more and more households use DVR technology, television as a marketing channel must use new media marketing strategies to build brands, consumer trust, and loyalty. Conversely, the more dollars spent on new media ads, the more they are starting to mirror the higher-end imagery of television ads.

Will the television advertising model go the way of the Internet? TiVo predicts more subscribers will opt for its branded content channels.

With this concept in mind, TiVo has developed a way for companies to use television as a marketing medium while still giving consumers absolute control over the content they watch. TiVo is hoping its new branded content television shows, called Product Watch, will be the answer to many television advertisers' frustrations.

TiVo will allow viewers to select from five branded categories — Automotive, Entertainment, Financial, Lifestyles, and Travel & Leisure. Once users subscribe to one of these categories, they will receive a branded show 1 to 60 minutes in length from one of their advertisers on a regular basis. The idea here is that just as on the Internet, if companies provide interesting and relevant information that isn't simply an infomercial, consumers will pay attention and subscribe to the branded content. As of April 2006, 10 percent of TiVo's 4.4 million users had opted in to the branded programming service (Kaye, May 2006).

Advertisers such as General Motors, LendingTree, Sony Pictures, Tourism Australia, and Kraft Foods have been among the first to jump on board. Advertising rates will most likely be based on a per-download basis, just as with most Internet marketing campaigns. With advertisements based on subscriptions and purchased per download, advertisers will see measurable return on investment and gain more insight to their audiences and what is working and what is not.

Rather than fighting new technology, many brands are now embracing new media channels in the television industry and seeing it as a more effective way to push new products and shows to an engaged audience. For example, *Desperate Housewives* and *Lost* are available online the day after the television episodes air. And unlike today's television, the online videos contain an ad or two that cannot be skipped over. In addition, advertisers are finding that showing their messages in a more interactive format rather than as a regular television commercial is more effective in getting consumers to take an intended action, such as shopping online.

Shift TV and OnlineTVRecorder.com, two German start-up companies, are offering what may be the future of the television industry. Both companies have signed deals with major German television companies to allow viewers to use their web browsers as devices to record whatever shows they want and watch them through a web-based interface or download them to a portable video device. Paying attention to these types of trends in new media now will help advertisers better adjust to future changes in traditional media channels.

Creating Television Shows and Commercials Exclusively for New Media Use

Nike is one of the major brands to truly embrace marketing in the new media by not only using new media to market its product, but actually incorporating new media technology into its product. But the creation of the new iPod-compatible running shoe isn't Nike's only new media contribution. In the spring of 2006 Nike developed JogaTV, aimed at providing a very targeted "Internet TV" channel for US soccer fans. Nike partnered with Google to develop the new Joga.com social networking site that allowed soccer fans to download a video application that enabled automatic downloads of new content of interest to soccer fans.

Nike's marketing channel was not only targeted to its soccer audience and younger, tech-savvy customers, it also provided an ultimate channel for word-of-mouth marketing — which, surprisingly, most large companies don't take advantage of. According to JupiterResearch, while 90 percent of large companies believe that customer recommendations and word of mouth are extremely important in influencing purchase decisions, only 33 percent of them are actively monitoring and implementing word-of-mouth campaigns — as opposed to 66 percent of small- and medium-size businesses (*eMarketer,* June 2006).

In 2006, Philips Electronics launched its new Norelco Bodygroom shaver for men. It did so on a limited budget, hoping to use viral marketing as the means of increasing sales. Understanding that the target audience of men aged 18 to 35 was likely to be online, the company created a commercial exclusively for the Internet. The commercial, which can be seen only at www.shaveeverywhere.com, uses Flash video to make the commercial as much like a television commercial as possible. The only difference is that it's a bit more risqué than your typical prime time television commercial. The commercial features a cheeky, overly confident man in a bathrobe talking about the "sensitive issues" of male body grooming and the importance of shaving places other than your face. The target audience, the limited budget, and the taboo subject of an all-over-body shaver made the Internet the perfect medium for pushing this product.

Because of the humorous nature of the ad, Philips was able to see the true power of online viral marketing. With limited support from online advertising, the shaveeverywhere.com site gained most of its traffic through word of mouth, including being mentioned on more than 1,000 blogs and getting 13,000 web links. The site itself received more than 900,000 visits in the first three weeks. This campaign is another example of great use of new media marketing, as the promotion not only increased buzz about the product but led to significant offline sales of the project.

Making Brand-Building Campaigns Viral

Based on a survey of US marketers carried out between December 2005 and January 2006, Osterman Research reported that the most influential factors in driving a word-of-mouth campaign are the type of customer service received (topping the list at 82 percent), followed by how newsworthy the information is and the price of the product (*eMarketer*, June 2006). Another contributing factor was how entertaining the campaign is. In the case of the entertaining Norelco Bodygroom commercial on the Internet, we can see that it produced some very rapid results.

The Miller Lite brand also used an entertaining angle in their 2006 "Man Laws" campaign on the web. The idea behind the new media marketing campaign was to encourage men to submit one-minute videos showing why they should become members of "Men of the Square Table." Visiting www.manlaws.com allowed visitors to see celebrities such as Burt Reynolds and other characters voting on "manly" laws such as how to clink bottles while toasting without sharing germs. (Hint: use the bottom of the bottle, not the top!) Even I, who am definitely not in their target audience, found a few of the video clips entertaining enough to forward to my beer-drinking male friends.

Miller Lite cleverly released a statement explaining that members must be able to "rule on everything from barbecue etiquette and lawn fertilizing to bolo ties and calling shotgun!" Winners had the opportunity to be flown to LA for a screen test and a chance to be on an actual Miller Lite advertisement. Site visitors could view recent entries and commercials featuring the Man Laws or submit their own laws. Having fun with new media content is an excellent way to generate consumer loyalty, strengthen your brand, and encourage word-of-mouth marketing.

References

Blackshaw, Pete. 2006. Kicking the World Cup Blog Ball? *ClickZ*, June 13.

Crowell, Grant. 2004. Public Relations via Search Engines. *ClickZ*, June 30.

Eisenberg, Bryan. 2006. Ruling the Roost: Word of Mouth, Part 1. *ClickZ*, June 23.

Hrastnik, Rok. 2006. Digging Deep To Get The Most From RSS Technology. *DEMC E-Magazine*, March 26.

Kaye, Kate. 2006. TiVo Offers Subscriptions to Branded Content. *ClickZ*, May 9.

____. 2006. Financial Firms Should Get Out and Socialize. *ClickZ*, June 30.

Lerma, Pete. 2006. March Madness, Again on Demand. *ClickZ*, March 21.

____. 2006. Participating in the Conversation. *ClickZ*, June 13.

Parker, Pamela. 2006. Study; 15% of Brand Searches Stray from Company's Site. *ClickZ*, April 17.

Stein, Gary. 2006. CGM as an Advertising Tactic. *ClickZ*, April 10.

Washburn, Judith H., Brian D. Till, and Randi Priluck. 2000. Co-branding: Brand Equity and Trial Effects. *Journal of Consumer Marketing* 17:7, December.

Wegert, Tessa. 2006. A Day in the Life of the Average Consumer. *ClickZ*, June 22.

CHAPTER EIGHT

IS YOUR WEBSITE READY?

Your website is the final and most important piece of a new media marketing campaign. This is the point in the campaign where customers take the action you have intended for them to take. Whether your goal is to have them purchase something from your website, provide you with their demographic information, or simply locate your nearest storefront, it is crucial that your website is user-friendly. Once your potential customers have come this far, you don't want to lose them. Ensuring that your website, microsites, or landing pages complement your marketing campaign and reinforce the desired "call to action" is critical at this point.

This chapter explores how to ensure that your website is ready to capture the response generated from the overall campaign, and how to essentially close the deal. This chapter also covers search engine optimization, which is essential to your overall online marketing success.

Remember the Basics of Good Web Design

Since the growth of the Internet, new technology and online fads have come and gone. And even the most talked-about marketing campaigns will only get visitors to your website once. After that, it's the content and design of your site that keeps people coming back for more and turning visitors into lasting customers.

Unless you are in the entertainment or technology industries, using the latest and flashiest web technology is not necessary for a successful web presence.

No matter how sophisticated Internet technology becomes, top-rated sites have always been the ones with the most up-to-date information and easiest navigation. Sites such as Google, Yahoo!, and Amazon continue to enjoy success because they are so easy to use. Yahoo! has simple graphics and a mostly text-based interface, but people log on again and again for its fast-downloading content and easy-to-use home page. Unless you're in the entertainment or technology industry, people are not expecting the newest web applications, heavy downloads, or audio and video clips. So, unless the use of flashy technology is an integral part of your overall marketing campaign — such as in the Norelco Bodygroom example discussed in Chapter 7 or the BMW films discussed in Chapter 6 — these elements really aren't necessary.

However, just as a great magazine cover or brochure captures users' attention with great images, photos, and well-written text, websites should be appealing. And most importantly, let visitors know right away, "What's in it for me?"

So many companies still make the mistake of using their home page as a platform to talk all about themselves, while in reality, customers really want to know, "How can *you* help *me*?" With that said, staff bios, company news, and history should never be on the home page. Keep this type of information in the "About the Company," "Press Room," or "Investor Relations" sections of your website. Save your home page for reinforcing your marketing message and encouraging visitors to take the actions you intend for them.

How can you tell if your website is capturing the interest of visitors? Simply take a look at your current website traffic report. Are significant numbers of people leaving immediately after reviewing the home page? Although the top exit page on most sites is in fact the home page, if the percentage is higher than 50 percent, I strongly recommend a redesign or putting more customer-centered incentives on the page to encourage them to click on to the desired pages of the site.

Use the following tips to ensure your website is user-friendly:

- *Get to the point.* New visitors should be able to find out exactly what your company/product can do for them in less than 15 seconds. Everything on your home page should help new customers make the decision to buy your product or take the specific action you intend.

- *Showcase new information and products on the home page.* Create a designated spot on your home page to showcase new content. By keeping new content in the same designated area, repeat visitors hoping to find the same information they found before won't be confused by it being in a different location. Also, it's a good idea to date new content; it not only encourages visitors to check back often, but also alerts search engines that your website provides the most up-to-date information. Search engines such as Google like to provide searchers with the newest information first, so providing a recent date can help give your site a boost in the rankings. Finally, updating a website is much cheaper than updating a brochure or any other type of print material. Take advantage of the web by using it to test new promotions.

- *Don't focus all your attention on the home page.* Remember that search engines can send visitors to any page of your site. Therefore special offers, incentives to sign up for email lists, and other important calls to action should be clear on every page.

- *Encourage viral marketing.* Whenever possible, remind visitors to pass the information on to their friends. Incentives such as "email this coupon to a friend and you'll both save $10" are effective in bribing people to spread the word. However, even a simple "email a friend" link has proven quite effective — especially for sites that provide useful news stories and how-to information.

- *Collect email addresses.* Create an environment that encourages users to give you their email addresses. Remember, creating a database of names and gathering information about your customer base is one of the reasons you drive people to your website in the first place. Give users an option to be included on your mailing list. Then email coupons, tips, and advice — anything that will spark some interest and keep them coming back for more.

(Keep reading for more ideas on building and using your email list later in Chapter 9.)

E-commerce Strategies from Amazon.com

If you want to see an example of a perfectly executed e-commerce site, buy something from Amazon.com. This site combines all the

Simplify the buying process: Fewer clicks to checkout mean more chances of completing the sale.

most effective technologies in e-commerce design, in one spot. These design features include the following:

1. **Site search feature**

   Having a user-friendly site search feature is essential to helping customers find what they are looking for fast. Even if you only have a few hundred products, a site search feature is always a good idea. Allow shoppers to search by keyword, brand, product category, or even price range. The more you can personalize the search to how they shop, the better.

2. **Personalization**

   Buy something from Amazon.com and you'll witness personalization technology at its best. Based on your past purchases or product views, you'll see recommended products throughout the shopping process on Amazon.com. After your purchase, you'll receive targeted emails with discounts to more related products. And when you return to Amazon.com, a personalized home page awaits you, suggesting more products you might like. The more you shop and browse, the more on-target these recommendations become. Because the products are so personalized to you, the emails and additional information feel helpful rather than intrusive.

3. **Customer reviews**

   Helping the customer through the buying process by not only providing detailed information about the product, but allowing other customers to provide honest testimonials, is a sure way to close a sale.

The Importance of Easy, Safe Checkout

Industry research shows up to 75 percent of shoppers abandon their online shopping carts before completing the checkout process. Therefore, making this process as smooth as possible is essential to completing the sale. There is a reason Amazon.com is famous for its "one-click shopping." The fewer the clicks to checkout, the better your chances are of closing the sale. Also, make it obvious to shoppers how to add to, save, or edit their orders. Providing pictures of the product during the "view cart" and "checkout" process, rather than just simple text descriptions, has also proven effective in closing the sale.

If you do have to have a long checkout process, it's a good idea to include a progress indicator on each checkout page. No matter how many steps are in your checkout process, let customers know where they are in the process. Number the steps and label the task clearly for each step. Give shoppers an opportunity to review what they did in previous steps and a way to return to their current step if they go back.

Another word of advice: Make the checkout process even easier for new visitors than registered customers. Acquiring new customers and making them trust your site is much harder than selling to the loyal ones. In other words, don't make new customers go through unnecessary steps to complete an order. Don't position registration and log-in as an obstacle between new visitors and checkout.

Another important strategy to decrease the number of people who abandon their shopping cart mid-checkout is to provide a link back to the product. That way, after an item is placed in the shopping cart, shoppers can easily jump back to make sure they selected the right item. For a good example, visit the Victoria's Secret website (www.victoriassecret.com), which provides not only text links but images of the products during the entire checkout process. Studies have shown that simply placing a thumbnail image of the product in the customer's cart during the checkout process increases conversions by as much as 10 percent!

Just as important as providing an easy checkout process is showing customers that your shopping cart is safe and their personal information will be secure when they shop with you. One way to give new customers confidence to do business with you is to provide your company's phone number and contact information at the bottom of each page. Not only is this essential if there is a problem during checkout, but it also helps instill more confidence in shoppers to see that there is a real company behind this online store — and therefore encourages them to complete the sale.

It is also a good idea to provide an alternate way to purchase your products, such as a form customers can print and fax or a telephone number to call in the order. Not all shoppers are comfortable using credit cards online.

Including an image of the product in the shopping cart during checkout can increase your conversion rate.

And finally, adding a third-party logo to your shopping cart — such as VeriSign, Better Business Bureau, or even credit card logos — helps give shoppers more confidence in your site. Showing a partnership or affiliation with an already trusted company helps your site look more credible to shoppers.

Consider your audience when providing payment options

In the US and Canada, the majority of online shoppers either pay by credit card or PayPal. However, if you are hoping to attract shoppers in other countries, it is important to understand how they prefer to use the Internet and which payment methods they are most comfortable with. According to a 2005 *eMarketer* report, Internet shoppers in the UK and France prefer payment methods similar to those in North America. However, 83 percent of German online shoppers use bank transfer as their number one method of payment. Shoppers in Italy and Spain are somewhat comfortable using all types of payment methods; however, PayPal ranks last on the list, with only 16 percent of Italians and 7 percent of Spanish using this method. Finally, almost all countries in the Asia Pacific prefer to pay by credit cards, bank transfers, and COD (cash on delivery), with very few using PayPal (Grau, July 2005).

The Right Way to Cross-Sell Online

Just as a sales clerk in your favorite department store may suggest a pair of shoes to match the new suit you are about to buy, displaying complementary products to customers shopping online is a great way to ensure a bigger final sale. Thanks to the latest in e-commerce technology, it's fairly easy to have products grouped to automatically display related products to customers during the shopping process.

Effective cross-selling online can be done in two different ways. The first way is to list products that complement each other. For example, recommending new speakers to go with a new stereo. The second way is to recommend products that are essentially the same, but are perhaps different brands or price points. That way, if the product displayed is missing a specific feature a shopper was hoping for or isn't quite right, the shopper can easily see something similar. For example, your site might say, "Here are some similar stereos you might like." A word of caution here: Recommending similar products should only be done during the product research phase.

Once a shopper puts an item in their cart and enters the checkout phase, pushing similar products to them will only make them reconsider their purchase. During the checkout phase it's best to showcase smaller price point items such as accessories or other items that tend to be impulse buys. Ensure these impulse buys can be easily added to cart. If a shopper is required to go back and choose a size or color before they can purchase the item, you will divert them from the checkout path.

Simple sites that emphasize text over graphics often rank best on the search engines.

Optimizing Your Website for Search Engines

As of the publication date of this book, Google continues to have the strongest hold on the search engine market, capturing more than 43 percent of the market share, followed by Yahoo! with more than 28 percent, and MSN with just over 12 percent. AOL and Ask hold just over 5 percent each, and the rest such as AltaVista, AlltheWeb, HotBot, Lycos, and Netscape hold less than 1 percent each (Sullivan, August 2006).

Top search engines partner up on occasion, use similar technologies, or even outsource specific searches to each other if their own technology doesn't produce adequate results. And just when you think you've got it all figured out, everything seems to change! It is a full-time job simply keeping up with all the nuances and changes in search technology. However, don't despair. The following guidelines include the standard strategies for optimizing your website for search engines. For best results, implement as many of these techniques as you can.

Search engines read text, not graphics

The most important thing to consider when optimizing your website for search engine success is that search engines read text, not graphics. Websites with Flash introductions or graphic-heavy home pages are at a disadvantage from the start. When it comes to top search engine rankings, simple sites that place an emphasis on text rank best.

Choose the right keywords

Keyword phrases are what Internet users type into a search engine to find relevant products and services. They are typically two to three words long.

Before spending the time to optimize your site, it's a good idea to use a program such as Wordtracker.com or Overture (now Yahoo! Search) to help you determine which keyword phrases have the highest search volume. That way you can make sure your efforts are spent optimizing for the *right* keywords. A service such as Word-Tracker.com is a paid service that not only gives you a breakdown of your keyword phrases by search volume, but goes a step further by telling you how much competition there is for each phrase. In this way, you can find the keyword phrase with the highest search volume and the least amount of competition.

Your home page and your tags

Once you have determined the best keywords to use, the next step is to put those keyword phrases within the content of your website. Pay extra attention to the first paragraph on your home page, as search engines most often read the first few lines of a site to determine its relevancy to a user's search. Use as many keywords and keyword phrases as possible in that first paragraph to ensure your site comes up when a user searches for those particular keywords. For example, on my husband's construction website, www.berkhome .com, we've packed the first few paragraphs with many important keyword phrases to help potential customers find his site:

Berkley Construction San Diego General Contractor

San Diego Home Remodeling, Property Improvements, Maintenance & Repair

Specializing in San Diego room additions and home remodeling, Berkley Construction General Contracting can help you maximize the value of your property. Whether the project requires interior or exterior home painting or a major home remodel, Berkley Construction can make the experience professional and affordable … Please browse our site for more information about our San Diego room additions and home remodeling services.

The home page text not only introduces the company's services, it also includes all of the keyword phrases that a potential customer might use when searching for a local general contractor. Turning the most competitive keywords into basic text links such as "San Diego room additions" and "home remodeling services" gives additional weight to these keyword phrases. Providing keyword-friendly text links as well as text-based navigation is an effective way to attract search engines and provide them with an entry point to index more pages of your site.

Next, you'll need to make sure your web designer included the appropriate tags in your HTML code that correspond with your website text. Remember, the more consistent your text and tags are, the more solid your ranking will be. Below I have included the types of tags that are important for search engine positioning, as well as a good example of what a tag should look like in your HTML code. Still using the Berkley Construction website as an example, you can see how all of the pieces match up. For example, important keywords such as "San Diego General Contractor" and "San Diego home remodeling" are repeated throughout.

Title tag

The title tag is the first sentence an Internet user will see when your website comes up in a search. Be sure your title tag includes both keywords and a solid marketing message that will encourage users to click to your site.

Example of a title:

Berkley Construction — San Diego Home Remodeling, Property Improvements, Maintenance and Home Repair

Example of description:

<meta name="description" content="We specialize in helping you increase property value through professional quality home remodeling, repair, painting and construction">

Meta tag

Meta tags are keywords and phrases inserted into the code of your web page that are not viewable to the user, but are viewable to the search engines. Most search engines use a technology called "spiders" or "web crawlers" to find and index web pages. Spiders crawl across your entire web page, making sure that meta tags match the regular text on your site. The more consistent your tags are with your actual site content, the better.

At one time, meta tags were a primary factor in ranking websites. Unfortunately, many website owners and marketers began taking advantage of the system and repeating the same keywords excessively throughout their meta tags — hoping to trick search engines into giving them higher ranking. The result was a less valuable search for the end user. For this reason, many of the top search engines — such as Excite and Lycos — quietly dropped this category from their search engine ranking technology while newer search engines such as Google and AlltheWeb never added this requirement at all.

"In the past, we have indexed meta keyword tags but have found that the high incidence of keyword repetition and spam made it an unreliable indication of site content and quality. We do continue to look at this issue and many re-include [meta tags] if the perceived quality improves over time," Jon Glick, AltaVista's director of Internet Search told Danny Sullivan, editor-in-chief of *ClickZ* (Sullivan, October 2002).

Although meta tags are not as essential to ranking as they were in the early 90s, it doesn't hurt to continue to implement them. My advice on meta tags is to add them anyway because smaller search engines may still pick them up.

Example of meta tags:

<meta name="keywords" content="san diego general contractor, home remodeling, san diego room additions, san diego construction, san diego painting, san diego home painting, san diego home remodeling, custom painting, faux finishing, tile, cabinet and counter installation, kitchen remodeling, san diego decks, custom decks, san diego construction project management">

Alt tag

Have you ever rolled your mouse over an image on a website and seen a box of text pop up? That text is called an alt tag. Alt tags identify by text what the image is. Since search engines don't read graphics, by adding alt tags, you are adding a text element that search engines can read. Alt tags allow all computers to know exactly what is on your site, regardless of what platform they are using. Technology such as Watchfire (www.watchfire.com) was designed with alt tags in mind so that people with disabilities can use the Internet. For example, a person with visual impairment who is using the Internet would have a special browser that reads the alt tags to let him or her know what is on that page. Therefore, it is especially important to include alt tags on your main navigation buttons so users with disabilities can know where to click to get their information.

Keep image tags brief. No more than a short phrase, long enough to include your keywords, but effective enough to actually describe your image to users with disabilities. To find out if your website is viewable by users with disabilities, search for websites that will quickly test your site, such as http://bobby.watchfire.com.

Example of alt tags:

<img src="office_building.gif" alt="Our San Diego Construction Office">

Redirects, pop-ups, and pop-unders

Redirects are a big red flag for search engines, mostly due to the pornography industry's abuse of the technology. If your URL redirects someone to another site automatically, the search engines assume you are hiding your real content, and therefore they will not rank you. Along with redirects, pop-ups and pop-unders can be equally devastating to your search positioning.

Back buttons

Search engines such as Yahoo! and Google will not sell ad space or keywords to websites that have disabled their browser "back" buttons. Other search engines are following suit, so keep back buttons active.

Text links

In addition to reading the text on your site, search engine spiders pay extra attention to text links. The more keywords you can put within your text links, the better. For example, rather than "Click here!" use this opportunity to add some keywords, such as "Click here for discount widgets." Search engines also look for text links to help them index your entire site. If your website only has graphic buttons for navigation, it will be very difficult for search engines to get past your home page and rank other pages within your site. Always add

Using text-based navigation, instead of Flash or Java, will help search engines index more pages of your site.

text-based navigation to your site. Text navigation can easily be added to the bottom footer of all pages within your site in addition to your regular, graphic-based navigation.

Site maps

Site maps are always a good idea. They not only help users find exactly what they are looking for, but they also help search engines index your website effectively, much in the same way text-based links do. Site maps are a way of outlining all the sections of your website in plain text. Search engines love site maps because they make categorizing each page and its content much easier. When creating your site map, link to as many specific product and service pages as possible within your site. In addition, be sure to link the entire product name, rather than adding a "click here" after the product name. This is the best way to help individual product and service pages get indexed by the search spiders.

Frames

Frames are a search engine's worst nightmare. Luckily most web designers today are aware of this, so few sites are being designed with frames. Frames are essentially two (or sometimes more) web pages embedded together. Search engines pull one page at time. So when a search engine is looking for information, it will pull pages out of their frame, causing loss of headers, footers, or important navigational features. Also, the way HTML code is written in frame-based websites hides the important content and keywords that search engines are looking for. Bottom line: Get rid of frames as soon as possible.

Flash pages, image maps, and heavy graphics

Websites that use a lot of heavy graphics or Flash animation have a hard time being recognized by the search engines. Ideally search engines like to see at least 200 words of related text. (In other words, text that matches your title tags, meta tags, and so on). Placement of your text is also key. Heavy graphics, animation, and JavaScript can push important text way down in the coding of your web page. To check how far down your home page text starts, simply, view your source code (right-click with your mouse and select "view source"). Are lengthy lines of JavaScript and other complex code pushing your important, keyword-loaded text toward the bottom of the page? If so, this could be hurting your rankings. To avoid this problem, opt for plain HTML text links rather than graphic and code-heavy image maps. Keep overall web page graphics light and keep important text toward the top of the page.

Flash pages simply cannot be read by search engines. However, Flash pages can be a very effective part of your website. Your best bet is to embed a small Flash movie within your regular HTML page. Or better yet, provide a simple HTML link to your Flash movie. Never make your home page designed entirely in Flash.

It's frustrating for web designers to learn that their innovative work and imagination won't be the first thing that captures users' attention when they visit a site. But it's the simpler sites that get the highest ranking on the search engines.

For some businesses, however, having a basic HTML home page doesn't make sense. In order to compete in your industry, maybe you need to show off your creative side. For example, if you are a graphic artist, an independent filmmaker, a cartoonist, or a musician, your website might benefit from a graphic-heavy or animated home page. If this is the case, I suggest you also focus your attention on the other optimization strategies such as link development.

Graphic-heavy and Flash-based sites can still achieve a good search engine ranking by placing an emphasis on attaining link popularity.

Link Popularity

Link development should be a large piece of your search engine optimization plan. Top search engines such as Google determine which website to rank highest by how many incoming links it has — in other words, how popular the website is. The theory is that if other websites think your site is important and credible enough to link to, then it may be worth ranking higher than the other sites. The key to building successful link popularity is paying attention to the quality of sites that provide links to you, rather than the quantity. In other words, if you can get a link from a major news website such as CNN.com or MSNBC.com that talks about your products and services, the link is weighted much more heavily than 100 links from small local businesses or hobby sites with no link popularity of their own. Taking time to build the right links is invaluable.

The first step in building a successful link-popularity campaign is to visit a site such as www.linkpopularity.com and see how many

Visit LinkPopularity.com to see how many websites are already linking to you. Then type in a competitor's URL to compare.

websites are already linking to you. Then enter a few URLs of your competitors' sites and see who is linking to them. This will give you a good idea of how many links you may need in order to beat them in the search engine ranking game. It will also give you some good insight into what kinds of partnerships and links they are getting, so you can see if it makes sense to contact those same websites.

Stay away from automated link exchange programs or webrings. The problem with these types of link development strategies is that Google will actually penalize a site with too many outgoing links. The idea is to have as many links as possible coming *to* your site, while limiting the number of links going out.

A great way to achieve this is by becoming a content provider in your industry. Offer to write articles or provide content for other news sources or websites in your industry in exchange for giving you a byline and link to your website within the article. Similarly, online press releases are a great way to fuel your overall link popularity. Write a keyword-friendly press release about your company, product, or service and submit it to major news and PR services such as Google News, PR Newswire, PRWeb, and others. (Review the tips in Chapter 7 regarding submitting an online release.)

Is Your Website Ready?

If writing isn't your strong suit, there are other link building options beyond writing articles and submitting press releases that are equally effective. Simply posting comments on other people's blogs with a link back to your site or even writing a product review where you audience is likely to be can help build your online visibility. However, the blog posts you submit or reviews you write must be on sites related to your industry, contain the keywords you want to be found for, and have a high amount of web traffic to be effective. You can visit Quantcast.com to determine how much traffic another site gets, as well as learn more about the audience that frequents that site.

Here is an example of how I used product reviews to help boost search ranking for the website TAAZ.com, a new virtual makeover website that allows women to simply upload a photo and try on makeup and hairstyles. In addition to the more standard search terms we wanted to be found for, like "virtual makeover," I also focused on more long tail search terms. These are searched terms that are more specific (often 3–5 words long) and often have far less search volume than the primary, shorter phrases. However, long tail search terms can be highly effective at driving extremely targeted traffic, as well as finding niche terms that your website can excel at. Plus people who type in longer, more specific search terms are more likely to convert because they are past the initial research phrase and know exactly what they are looking for.

One strategy for boosting traffic via the search engines during the fall was to focus on the top searched Halloween costumes, and to show women how they could use TAAZ.com to find the right makeup for that costume. Step 1 included using Wordtracker.com to determine the list of top searched Halloween makeup. We learned that "fairy makeup," "pirate makeup," and "vampire make-up" were among the top searches. Step 2 involved creating a search engine friendly article about how to apply each type of makeup. In step 3, we strategically sought out links back to these Halloween in-spired makeup tips in order to build link popularity. We discovered the PartyCity.com and BuyCostumes websites already had a top ranking on Google for these search phrases. In Step 4, we posted customer reviews under appropriate costumes that said things along the lines of, "I love this vampire costume. I even found the perfect makeup to match at TAAZ.com, the new virtual makeover site that lets you try on makeup before you buy it."

The tactic helped increase TAAZ.com's search ranking because first, it gave us a link from a popular website, and second, because the link included keywords that we wanted to be found for. The extra added benefit comes from the actual person who reads the re-view — we have reached them in a very targeted way, and they are therefore more likely to want to check out our site and see what it is about.

A similar SEO link building tactic revolves around high traffic sites like Yahoo! Answers. Yahoo! Answers is a place where anyone can ask and answer questions. As a business, if you can answer ques-tions related to your product or industry, you can not only find a new costumer, but the activity and link back to your site from such a popular portal, will also help your SEO ranking. Plus, due to the growing popularity and depth of information now on Yahoo! Answers, many of these questions and answers themselves show up as top search results.

If you go to Answers.yahoo.com and customize your own feed by keywords (click on the Advanced tab at the top of the page and follow the steps) you will be notified each time a question related to your topic or product arises. This way you can answer it, assert your expertise in the field and increase your online visibility. While working with TAAZ.com, we had an intern specifically dedicated to monitoring questions such as "Which hairstyle looks best on me?" or "How do I find the right make up colors." Our intern would simply answer the post and introduce them to TAAZ.com, as a great way to try the hairstyle or makeup on their own photo.

For best results with search engines, implement as many of the above strategies as possible. Many search engines follow a combination of these guidelines to determine ranking. The more your site content matches your site title and your site meta tags, and so on, the better your chance of holding a solid ranking with the top engines. And the longer you hold these consistently, the higher your ranking will go.

How Long Does Getting to the Top Take?

Getting to the top of the search engines is not an overnight process. In fact, even the most effectively optimized websites can end up in a "holding period" for several months before search engines will even index them. Many search engine marketers refer to this holding period as the "sandbox theory" (the sites are placed in a sandbox where they can all play nicely away from the real sites).

Google applies the sandbox theory to all websites launched after March 2004. Despite how well optimized a site is, websites launched after that date do not often rank well for their first few months live on the Internet. New websites are often placed on probation — and their rankings are kept lower than expected in searches — prior to being given full value for optimization. The sandbox practice was implemented for a few different reasons, primarily to make it difficult for search engine spammer sites to get ranked. Google wants to give more weight to long-term sites that will still be around in a year, rather than sites that latch onto the latest search engine ranking tactic and essentially try to "cheat" their way to the top.

While all types of sites can be placed in the sandbox, the problem appears much more frequently for new websites seeking rankings for highly competitive keyword phrases and for sites that repeat specific keyword phrases too often (which can be considered search engine spam).

Once your site is in the sandbox, only time can get it out. However, there are a few ways to speed up the process. These steps all go back to good website optimization, including strong keyword-friendly content and a solid link development strategy. It's also a good idea for business owners with new domain names to get a basic site launched right away, rather than waiting for the site to look perfect or be completely finished. Even a basic information page that lets users know that a full site will be launching soon will help shorten the overall wait time before your site is out of the sandbox.

Paying for Positioning

Waiting several months to get picked up by the search engines can cost you customers. Fortunately, there are now ways to jump ahead of the line with "pay-per-click positioning." Search engines such as Yahoo!, MSN, and Google allow advertisers to buy keywords to ensure that their company listing will show up whenever that word is searched.

It's hard to say just how much you should spend on keywords per month. This is something that varies with each industry and depends on what you wish to accomplish online. Search engine keywords are usually sold on a CPC (cost per click-through) basis. Pricing is then based on the popularity of the word, which is why I recommend choosing keywords that are as specific as possible. The more general the word, the more expensive it will be. Plus, general words earn a lot of wasted clicks from people not looking for your product specifically.

Let's go back to the real estate example. The keyword phrase "real estate" is an extremely expensive one, and unless you work for Century 21 buying keywords for its global office's website, there is really no reason to purchase this keyword. A local real estate agent is better off buying a more specific keyword phrase, such as "San Diego home for sale."

Using landing pages

It's a good idea to specify a unique URL with your keyword buy. This will ensure your visitors will immediately find exactly what they are looking for. Customized web pages designed to close the sale are called "landing pages." By creating pages specific to what the user is searching for, and then testing various offers and text on those pages, your conversion rate will be higher than if users are just led to your home page. Purchasing keywords is the most effective ad buy available, but it is easy to waste a lot of money if you don't take the extra steps to customize the results users will see when they click through to your site.

Writing effective ad copy

Just as important as the keywords you buy is the ad copy you include with that keyword. Both Google and Yahoo! allow advertisers to specify the ad copy or title tag that will appear when a keyword is searched. By customizing your ad copy to specific keywords, you will maximize your chance of quality click-throughs.

Once you are a regular advertiser with Google or Yahoo!, you can edit your keywords, ad text, and URLs as often as you like — which means you can run different keyword campaigns at different times of the year or month, or even daily. For example, if you buy the keyword phrase "bridesmaid dress," you can run the descriptive text "50 percent off on all bridesmaid dresses in July," which can take the person to a landing page with the coupon.

Promotions and coupons help your listing stand out from the rest. But be careful not to overuse punctuation or capital letters. Neither Google nor Yahoo! will accept ad copy that contains too much hype. Paid listings are meant to be read like editorial content, not advertisements. Therefore, your ad copy will be rejected if you use superlative words such as "best." Also, if you choose to use an offer or promotion as your ad copy, it must be a legitimate offer. Google won't let you use the word "free" unless your landing page actually gives away something for free. And if it's a "buy one, get one free" type of promotion, you must specify this before the person clicks. In other words, no misleading ads.

If you think you've seen ads on Google or Yahoo! that break these rules, it's because once you are a regular advertiser, your ads can go live instantly after you post an edit. But be assured that as soon as the search engine staff get a chance to review your ad copy, it will be pulled if it doesn't follow the guidelines. The pay-for-positioning guidelines are just that, guidelines. They are constantly changing to make the buys most effective for both searchers and marketers, so be sure to read the latest rules posted on Google and Yahoo! before you write your ad copy.

To sum up: Gaining new web traffic is more than adding the right tags and registering for the right search engines. It is a combination of all of the ideas and concepts outlined in this book to expand your overall web presence. Websites such as Google and Yahoo! recognize the most popular websites and tend to rank them higher over time. Google and Yahoo! determine a website's popularity by how many other quality websites are linked to it. In the end, the more web content you exchange with others in your industry and the more product links you get on other sites, the more this will help your overall web traffic. The more places your website address is found on the Internet, the better your chances of being found by the search engines.

There are entire books dedicated to designing effective websites and optimizing them for the search engines; however, the tips in this chapter are designed to provide you with workable guidelines to complement your overall new media campaign. The next chapter offers ways to optimize your email marketing strategies.

References

Aaronson, Jack. 2006. Effective Cross-Selling Online. *ClickZ*, June 2.

Crowell, Grant. 2006. Understanding Searcher Behavior. *ClickZ*, June 14.

Grau, Jeffrey. 2005. Western Europe E-commerce. *eMarketer*, December.

Sherman, Chris, and Danny Sullivan. 2006. Getting *The New York Times* More Search Engine Friendly. *ClickZ*, June 15.

Smith, Julian. 2006. Mobile Marketing: The Time's Right to Get a WAP Site. *ClickZ*, August 29.

Sullivan, Danny. 2006. ComScore. Media Metrix Search Engine Rankings. Search Engine Watch. August 21.

Sullivan, Danny. 2002. Death of a Metatag. *ClickZ*, October 1.

Thomases, Hollis. 2006. Surveying Agencies about Online Video Advertising. *ClickZ*, June 20.

CHAPTER NINE
FINE-TUNING YOUR EMAIL MARKETING STRATEGIES

One way to measure the success of a new media marketing campaign is by how many email addresses it collects. Since the growth of the Internet, email marketing has become one of the most cost-effective marketing components for companies of all sizes. Whether it's Business to Business (B2B) or Business to Consumer (B2C), email marketing allows you to improve customer service and increase brand loyalty by keeping your company in the forefront of customers' minds. According to a Summer 2008 survey by E-consultancy and R.O.EYE, online retailers worldwide agreed that email was second only to paid search (PPC) campaigns for increasing volume. A similar study in January 2008 by Radar Research discovered that four out of ten companies that advertised on search engines via PPC said email marketing gave them the best return on investment, more so than any other interactive marketing tactic (*eMarketer*, 2008). When done correctly, permission-based email marketing can outperform every other type of online marketing strategy. However, as discussed throughout this book, no single piece of a marketing campaign can stand alone. A great email newsletter must have the website to back it up and enough interest to build up your email list in the first place.

Email is the number one activity of Internet users, which is why email can be such an effective marketing tool. According to a 2002 Yankee Group survey, 72 percent of Americans are online, and of

Internet users spend more time reading and sending emails than on other online activities.

that group, 93 percent regularly check email from home and 85 percent check email from work. Of these Internet users, most say they would rather receive marketing messages via email than be disturbed at dinnertime with a phone call. They are also more likely to look at the messages in their inboxes than at junk mail stuffed in their home mailboxes.

Permission-Based Email Marketing

The key to an effective email marketing campaign is to make it permission-based only. In other words, your customers must "opt in" or choose to be on your email list. Never buy or rent an email list. Buying or renting a list is the same as sending out spam. No matter what an email list company may tell you about its subscribers, I guarantee that 99.9 percent of the people on those lists did not opt in to getting their email addresses and personal information sold. Sending email to people who did not personally request information from your company is spam, period. Spam cheapens your company brand and takes away consumer trust. Just as with your website traffic, the key with email is *quality* of leads, not quantity. So take the time to build your own email list. It will be invaluable. In fact, a 2008 Email Marketing Metrics Report by MailerMailer found that consistently, across all industries, the larger the email list, the lower the open and click rates of the email blast. Keep it up to date with relevant contacts who want to hear from you.

Generating a quality email list takes some time, but in the end, you'll have a captive audience that is truly interested in your product. But remember, when a customer offers you a private email address and demographic information, that person is trusting you. Don't abuse that trust.

Provide a privacy policy on your website promising not to sell customers' information to any outside parties or vendors. Let your customers know exactly what type of messages they should expect and how often. Also let them know that they have the option to unsubscribe from your list at any time. This will give customers confidence to register for your email newsletter.

If you do a joint promotion or co-branding effort with another website or company, don't exchange email lists. Instead, simply put that company's information in your newsletter. The emails should always come directly from you. If it looks like you have sold your customers' valuable information to another company, your customers will lose trust and unsubscribe from your list — and may well refuse any future contact with your company.

When enticing people to join your list, don't ask for too much personal information too early on. Just as you wouldn't ask someone you meet at a cocktail party for their home address and household income, asking for that much personal information before gaining mutual respect and trust is offensive online. Start by only asking for an email address and name. Be patient. Just as with friendships, it takes time get a clear picture of who your best customers are and what exactly they want out of your newsletter and website. You can get more personal information with future marketing efforts and promotions.

If your company appears trustworthy (that is, it is not going to sell customers' information), it will not be difficult to gather email addresses. Something as simple as sponsoring a contest or giveaway will work: "Enter to win a free [*insert your product here*]." Or offer a coupon or discount: "Subscribe to our newsletter and get 10 percent off your next purchase." Even offering content will work: "Join our newsletter for weekly tips on using our product. "

The most successful list-growth strategies include ongoing coupon incentives (for example, a monthly offer available only via email) and ongoing contests.

Offering coupons and free services isn't the only way to get customers to join your email list. Great website content can be enough incentive.

Focus on Content

Great content is a very effective incentive as well. Offering ongoing tips or useful advice related to your product or services establishes your company as an authority in your field and keeps customers interested. For example, at Vantage Internet, we send out a monthly newsletter to clients. It's full of strategies and tips for generating more sales online or getting more traffic to their websites.

Don't include company history, company news, or "about us" information in your newsletter unless it is being sent to investors. The truth is, your customers don't care about what's happening in your company — they care about how you can help them. Great content is anything that will interest your customers. And just like your home page, your newsletter has only seconds to capture a customer's attention before it ends up in the trash. Tell visitors right away what you can do for them and why they should choose your company.

Another strategy to keep customers opted in and interested in your email newsletters is to keep the material tight, short, and to the point. Short means maximum 500 words and no more than five regular departments. Most people don't like to read long emails, and if your newsletter has multiple departments it will be harder for you to keep it updated. This could hurt your ability to send newsletters consistently and provide solid new information. Another reason for keeping your email newsletters short is that if you provide too much information in the initial email, customers won't click through to your website. If they don't click, you will have no way to track the success of your campaign (unless you are emailing a printable coupon or have some other way of offline tracking). What sets online marketing apart from traditional marketing methods is the ability to track campaigns right down to the image people click on to buy your product. If your emails don't encourage people to click, you won't be able to track what part of your email campaign is working.

I learned this important tip when I sent out a very thorough email newsletter detailing a whole new line of Guayabera Mexican shirts for a client. The email listed all nine of the new shirts, complete with a picture, description, and price. The email generated a disappointing 5 percent click-through rate, and only a 2 percent sales rate. The following month, I sent my traditional newsletter with a small section titled "Take 10 percent off all Guayabera shirts! Click here to see our new line." I used only one picture of our most popular shirt and didn't include any information on price. I got a 40 percent click-through on that image alone! Less is more when it comes to email marketing. Entice them to click.

Timing Is Important

Next, determine the appropriate frequency (daily, weekly, monthly) and delivery time (Monday morning vs. Friday afternoon) for your email newsletter. Because I am an Internet marketing consultant, I check my email all day long. Therefore, it's appropriate for email newsletters regarding new marketing products and tips to come to me every day. However, if the other e-newsletters I subscribe to (for example, those from Amazon or Travelocity) came every day, I would be overwhelmed and would unsubscribe immediately. Instead, when I get an occasional email from Amazon about a new book I might be interested in or an email from Travelocity about a great fare to New York City, I am much more likely to take the time to read it and react. Just like an email from a distant college friend, it feels a bit more special when it only comes occasionally and contains something specific.

A local San Diego website emails its events calendar every Wednesday night. It arrives in time for the weekend but with enough time to forward it to all your friends whom you want to invite to local concerts and events.

At Jenny Craig, we found it most effective to send out emails every Monday morning. This was right after the weekend, when most dieters had strayed from their meal plans. Mondays proved an effective time to give words of encouragement and new promotions about Jenny Craig to help dieters through the week. For those dieters who needed extra encouragement, we also gave the option of daily "diet tips" emailed to them. The diet-tip emails were one to two sentences long: short enough for customers to read every day but long enough to keep Jenny Craig in the forefront of the customer's mind every day. (By the way, we wrote all 365 diet tips ahead of time and sent them out on an automated email system.)

The 2008 MailerMailer report found that Sunday is the newest day of the week to garner the highest open rates. Probably because more people are trying to get a head start on the work week, and checking their email on Sunday night — a time that is often uncluttered with other emails. According to the same report, Monday is the next best day, with open rates declining as the week goes on.

However these stats are the average, and it's important to note that appropriate frequency and timing differ from industry to industry. For example most restaurants and entertainment venues see higher open and click rates later in the week. If it isn't obvious when the best time to deliver your email is, just ask. When customers subscribe to your email list, ask them how often they would like to hear from you. Or, send email letters out different days of the week to see if there is a distinct difference in how many people actually respond. Looking at the averages is another good way to determine when you should send your email newsletter. According to a 2005 Response Rate Study by ExactTarget, on average, Friday is the best day of the week to actually get email read, while Sunday is the best day for click-throughs (Stewart, 2005).

Establish newsletter content based on your subscriber profiles. Most email list services will let you set up your subscription page so that users can specify which type of content they would like to receive from you. For example, for our client BowlersDepot.com we

Diet-related emails were opened most frequently on Mondays; local event emails were forwarded to more friends on Thursdays. When's the best time to send out your email message?

let users choose to be emailed "Discounts and Coupons," "New Product Information," or "Bowling Tips." We took it a step further to try to learn more about our audiences by offering "Senior Specials," "Military Specials," "Beginners Specials," and "Advanced Bowler Specials." By seeing how many people signed up for each list, we knew how much interest there was for each category and which areas to expand on. It also gave us more leverage to work out co-branding opportunities with related companies and in turn further expand our subscriber base. For example, by seeing how many people opted for "Senior Specials," we were able to approach other websites where this audience was likely to be and exchange banner ads on each other's email newsletters or do joint promotions to encourage more sign-ups. When you are able to truly track and identify your website's audience, it opens up some very cost-effective bargaining and ad swapping opportunities.

Leni Chauvin, a professional success coach and email marketer (www.attractclientsgalore.com), sums up her approach to email newsletters as follows:

> The secret for me is not to attempt to sell or push my services at all. All of my efforts go into publishing a first-class newsletter full of information that people want. This has served me well in establishing myself as an expert in my field. The newsletter is then forwarded to friends and colleagues around the word. Last count it was in 68 countries! It all boils down to "attracting vs. selling."

That is really great advice. If your newsletter offers something of true value, your subscriber base will increase and your company's online brand will grow. People are much more likely to forward an interesting newsletter to their friends and family than a hard sales pitch. Establish yourself as an expert in your industry by providing your subscribers with the important information they are looking for, and they will begin to see you and your company as the only source for this type of information and service.

However, no matter how important your newsletter content may be, it doesn't guarantee that your subscribers will read it. In fact, there is only one way to ensure that your emails don't end up in the trash: Write a great subject line!

Write a Great Subject Line

It's a shame that many legitimate offers and great newsletters aren't even read simply because the marketer didn't take the time to write an effective subject line. (*After all, it's only a few words,* the thinking goes. *How important can that be?*)

With more and more emails cluttering up all of our inboxes daily, it's more important than ever to write a great subject line. In fact, your subject line is one of the most important features of your email marketing efforts. It makes the first impression. It's these few words that either entice a potential customer to click on or delete the whole thing.

Spend a disproportionate amount of time working on your subject line. After all, if your message ends up in the trash, it won't matter how good your newsletter content was.

When writing subject lines, follow these tips:

1. **Keep them short and direct**

    Subject lines with less than 35 characters have a significant advantage. As subject lines increase, the open rate decreases. Most email browsers won't let users see past five or six words anyway, so long subject lines get lost. Don't waste space with fluff adjectives like "very." Use sturdy, descriptive words.

2. **Stress the benefits to the recipient**

    Make it easy for your potential customers to know exactly why they would benefit from reading your newsletter. There should be an instant reward or benefit for opening your message. A reward can be as simple as important information. Hinting at business results, such as "save time" or "earn money," is also effective. Tease readers by telling them just enough to make them want to click and find out more.

3. **Ask a question**

    Ask a question that sparks curiosity and teases the reader to want to know more. Also, asking a question makes the message sound more like a colleague's email, so it's more likely to be opened.

Take time to review what's currently in your inbox. Which subject lines encourage you to open the email and read on?

4. Write in a personal style

Never send an email to "undisclosed recipients" or provide a generic auto-response email address as the sender. These two things scream spam. The "To" field should only contain the recipient's name and email address (a bulk email program should allow you to send emails individually), and always use a company name or real person's name as the sender. A good rule to follow is that if you have a recognizable company name, use it; if not, use your own name. An update: Personalizing the subject line with the recipient's name used to be a good tactic used by marketers. However as more consumers become more internet savvy, and fear opening emails, characterized as spam, they are less likely to open emails that contain their name in the subject line. It just looks too much like spam. Whenever possible, write in a personal style. For example, "You're invited to our grand opening," but without necessarily including the recipient's name.

5. Tie in seasonal events or holidays

Tying in an upcoming holiday or seasonal event with your subject line is very effective. For example, "Save money on your Christmas shopping," "Go back to school in style with these tips," or "Lose 10 pounds before spring break."

6. Don't use the word "free"

The same rule applies to "Limited offer," "Buy now," or other hard sales terms. Many companies and ISPs will filter out emails with such words in the subject line to avoid bogging down their systems with spam. For example, a subject line with the word "guaranteed" will be blocked by the Road Runner Internet service provider. Also, be careful not to use too much hype, such as multiple exclamation marks or all caps. It sounds like spam and can be eliminated by ISP filters.

Creating a successful e-newsletter comes with practice. Each industry expects different things from a newsletter, and different formats work better for different types of businesses. Some of us have customers who are more computer literate than others; some have fast Internet connections while others are still on dial-up. Some check email every day at work, while others only check once a week from home. Knowing who your audience is is essential to creating and sending effective email marketing messages.

I am fairly confident that you have a flood of personal emails, business questions, jokes, spam, junk mail, and maybe even a couple of viruses in your email inbox right now. Take a moment to examine which emails entice you to read on and which ones you automatically delete. Of the marketing emails you do open, which ones encourage you to click through to that company's website? Which email newsletters did you actually subscribe to and why? Getting ideas from your own inbox is a great way to start building ideas for your own business email communications.

Six Easy Steps for Complying with the CAN-SPAM Act

Most US businesses have heard of the CAN-SPAM Act and its attempts to put an end to spam. Although the exact words may vary from state to state, the existing antispam law does recognize the need for you to send emails to people you have a pre-existing business relationship with and those who have requested your email communications. The following guidelines, along with your lawyer's advice, will help ensure that your email marketing strategies comply with the latest antispam laws.

1. **Be honest**

   Don't provide any misleading or false information. This means that your email subject line must accurately let customers know what they will find within the email message, should they decide to open it. Your sender line must be a real person, with a real return email address. Your offer must be legitimate; in other words, you can't promise "Click here for a free widget" and have the customer land on a page that says, "If you purchase three widgets, then you get one free." This is false advertising.

2. **Provide valid, physical contact information**

   All commercial emails must now contain a physical address, not just an email address and website.

3. **Don't send email to people who did not request to hear from you**

   As discussed earlier, taking time to build your own email list of people who actually want to hear from you will not only ensure that you are abiding the law, but will also give you a much higher return on investment in your email marketing.

4. **Do not buy or rent email lists**

   Email sent to a purchased list is always going to be considered spam. You can no longer use the excuse, "But they told me these people opted in … " Under the law, CAN-SPAM holds advertisers and everyone involved in sending the message accountable. If you send emails to people who did not request them, you must provide a clear notification that the message is commercial. This can be done by either putting "ADV" in the subject line or a simple line of text at the bottom; for example, "You are receiving this email because you opted to receive offers and information from XYZ company (list owner)."

5. **Keep your list up-to-date**

   If your customer list is more than one year old, the line gets a bit fuzzy on whether it is considered spam or not. To be on the safe side, be sure to update your list at least once a year.

6. **Always provide an opt-out option**

   Even if your customers did ask to be on your email list at one time, this does not give you the right to send promotional emails to them forever. You must always include an opt-out or unsubscribe option on all emails, and honor those opt-outs by removing them from your list right away.

The State of Email Marketing

Recent reports have discussed the decline in overall open rates, and a trend moving away from email marketing. I disagree with these reports. I am a strong believer that email marketing is the most cost-effective way to communicate with your customers and increase repeat business and viral marketing potential. With that said, there are a few reasons that could account for the decline in open rates. The first explanation for the decrease is that more people have started using email programs that disable automatic image downloading by default. Popular email programs like Hotmail force users to select "show content" or "mark as safe" in order to see the images in HTML messages. According to MailerMailer, "In order to track open rates, HTML messages contain a 1x1 pixel invisible image. When a recipient enables images to display when they read the message, the sending servers are able to track when the images was displayed and by whom — this is the 'open rate' information you see in your report. When images are blocked, the 'open' cannot be tracked."

Another cause for open rates becoming less accurate is that more people are reading their email through mobile devices, like smartphones. When viewing your email "on the go" you are less likely to download all the images, and simply view the text of the email. The fact that more people check their email on the go also accounts for the 2008 MailerMailer discovery that nearly one-third of opens occur within the first 2 hours after the send, with most opens happening between 4–6 hours. This means that most marketers will receive a majority of their customer responses from an email blast within 48 hours, making the time of day you send your message an even more important factor than before. This Christmas, I received emails from The Gap and Party City, sending time-sensitive emails promoting specials going on in their brick-and-mortar stores only. This shows that email is not only a great tactic to encourage people to your online store, but can also be used as a way to encourage shoppers to visit your offline store, while they are away from their work or home computer. After all, most of us are checking our email on the go, anyway.

The above stats regarding the majority of opens occurring in the first two days, was accumulated by reviewing the stats of many different companies in a variety of industries. It is important to note that different businesses may experience great results that do not happen in the first few hours or days. Most consumers today have at least two email accounts; one for their work related messages, and one for personal. Personally, in addition to my numerous work-related email addresses, I have a Hotmail account, that I specifically use for any type of online purchases that I make or non-work related websites I subscribe to. I do not check this email account every day, or even every week. But when I do check it, I am in the mood to shop! I typically look there first for special deals and incentives when I know I have a gift to buy or a trip to plan. I scan through all the email subject lines to find the best deals that have been delivered to my Hotmail account throughout the month. I have noticed this similar trend in delayed conversion on many of my email marketing clients. Those B2B clients who are sending business related information, products, or services tend to go directly to people's work email addresses, and therefore response is more immediate. However, those clients in the B2C category that are sending retail, beauty, entertainment, diet, or other non-business related emails tend to see a longer delay in results, since people more often use alternate email addresses to subscribe to these newsletters and promotions. Although open rates are declining, click rates have remained steady ... which shows that people are still clicking, even if open rates aren't being tracked as consistently and accurately. Further, as a result of the mobile devices people use to check email, it makes the timing of your email send more important than ever. Following the rules outlined in this chapter, and testing to perfect the right content and timing of your email blasts will provide your business with a low-cost way to generate more traffic and sales to your site.

As your marketing efforts progress, you will continue to fine-tune the email marketing elements covered in this chapter. In the next chapter, you'll learn how to measure the results of your new media marketing efforts, so you can determine just what areas of your campaign need to be modified in order to provide your company with the best return on investment for your marketing dollars.

References

Chauvin, Leni. 2003. Personal communication.

DiGuido, Al. 2004. Four for '04. *ClickZ*, January 15.

Grau, Jeffrey. 2005. Western Europe E-commerce. *eMarketer*, December.

Mullen, Jeanniey. 2006. Growing Your E-mail Database. *ClickZ*, June 26.

Soltoff, Paul. 2004. CAN-SPAM: The Reality. *ClickZ*, January 12.

Stewart, Morgan. 2005. Email Marketing: 2005 Response Rate Study. *ExactTarget*.

____. 2008. Consumers Opening Fewer Emails. *eMarketer*. November 14.

____. 2008. Email Marketing Metrics Report. *MailerMailer*. November.

CHAPTER TEN

MEASURING THE RESULTS

Before I even begin a new media campaign for a client, we sit down and determine what would define a successful campaign. For example, is the customer hoping to achieve more information about existing customers? Perhaps they are interested in simply attaining more overall web traffic. Are they looking to increase brand awareness, media coverage, and a higher search engine ranking? Or perhaps the goal of the campaign is simply to get direct sales. Determining the goals of the campaign will help you know which tools to implement as well as how to determine if the campaign was cost-effective.

Web Traffic Reports

The most basic ways to measure the success of new media campaigns is by referring to website traffic software. Google Analytics (which is free), Urchin, LiveSTATS, WebTrends, DeepMetrix, and NetTracker are all great software used to monitor your website's traffic. From these reports, you can see important information such as how many people are visiting your website each month, where the traffic is coming from, and even what keywords people used to find your site on the search engines. You will also be able to tell which pages are generating the most interest, as well as which pages cause people to leave your site. All of this information is important to monitor when determining which ad buys, promotions, content, or

Eighty-five percent of online shoppers end up making their purchases offline. This can make tracking the conversion rate difficult.

marketing strategies are most effective. However, as new media campaigns get more complex and marketers combine more offline marketing channels into the mix, tracking overall campaign success can be a bit trickier. Company goals and measures of success are also different from industry to industry. While one company may find concrete measurements of determining success by looking at average cost-per-click, another company may find this information completely irrelevant to their bottom line. Therefore your measurements of success should be customized to your own company goals and long-term as well as short-term business strategies.

Looking at Averages

Although each company has different goals and therefore different ways to measure success, looking at some industry averages is a good starting point. For example, according to *Practical eCommerce Magazine*, an e-commerce site with 6 to 9 percent of its visitors making purchases is considered a success, with 1 to 2 percent being the industry standard. For lead-generation sites, conversion rates in the high teens are considered successful, while the average lead-generation site converts approximately 5 or 6 percent of visitors (Greenfield, July 2006).

The above percentages represent average online conversions and do not show the number of conversions that may have occurred at a later date or offline. In today's world, these numbers are just as important to consider when determining the success of a new media campaign because most consumers use the Internet for research before they make a purchase decision, even when the actual purchase is made offline or at a later date. Although it can be difficult to accurately track the effectiveness of online marketing in generating offline sales, this chapter will give you an overview of common ways you can test and track the results of your marketing campaigns — as well as tips to improve your results.

Tracking Delayed or Offline Conversions

According to JupiterResearch, in 2005, 85 percent of online shoppers used the Internet to research products they then purchased offline. In fact, JupiterResearch went on to predict that more than half of all retail transactions will be influenced by the Internet by 2010. Similarly, comScore reported that during a study of online shoppers, only 37 percent purchased online, while 63 percent did online research but completed their transactions either by visiting a retail store or ordering by telephone (Stelter, April 2006).

The primary reason consumers turn to the Internet before making an offline purchase is for price comparison. The secondary reason is to find information to solidify their purchase decision — such as customer reviews, testimonials, or additional product information.

With that said, unless your business solely operates online, you cannot simply depend on off-the-shelf website traffic software to provide an accurate view of the success of your new media marketing efforts. In many cases, the best solution may be to hire a professional Internet consultant to implement a customized lead capture solution, which can significantly increase the number of leads generated from your new media marketing efforts. Lead capturing tools help you close more sales and track your website's effectiveness, and they keep you informed on which online marketing activities are giving you the best return on investment. These tools can also provide your marketing team with valuable insight about who your customers are by providing detailed demographic information. Depending on how your company collects leads or closes sales, much of the information can either be automatically collected from online sources or manually entered.

I once consulted for a highly competitive student loan consolidation company that combined Internet marketing with offline marketing campaigns including direct mail and telemarketing. All the leads, whether generated online or offline, were tracked in one online lead capture database. In addition, the database also tracked which leads turned into actual customers. In this way, we could tell exactly which marketing methods were proving most effective in not only generating leads but producing leads that turned into customers. The database was customized to include details about where each lead came from and how much that particular marketing element cost, so we could accurately measure our average cost-per-lead and cost-per-sale by specific campaign. And since we had already determined the cost-per-lead the company was prepared to pay, we were able to know whether each campaign was cost-effective or not — a true measurement of success.

It's a good idea to require an email address before awarding a coupon because then you can keep in contact with the potential customers, even if they don't redeem the coupon.

Like the student loan company mentioned above, many industries experience delayed conversion. This means that even though a lead is generated online, the actual sale or conversion can occur at a much later date. This is standard for industries such as real estate and mortgages, where it can take several months from the initial contact to close a sale. This is why keeping in contact with that lead through channels such as email marketing is so important to keep the lead hot. With such a long sales cycle, customers can easily get distracted and end up doing business with another company that captures their attention closer to the time when they are actually ready to make the purchase.

For a standard retail store, a printable coupon is an easy way to measure the direct sale generated from an online lead. If you are driving traffic to your site through multiple marketing campaigns, be sure to create a separate landing page with a unique coupon design or code for each campaign so you can track which marketing efforts lead to bringing each customer in the door. For example, have your pay-per-click campaign directed to a slightly different coupon than the banner ad campaign you may be running. In addition, it's a good idea to make visitors join your email list before they can download coupons. This way, if they don't redeem the coupon, you can at least start marketing to them in the hope that your next promotion may give them a bigger incentive to drop by.

Continuing to test different promotions and tracking how they affect both your email list and direct sales is important for measuring the success of a campaign. For example, you may find that although one promotion led to more sales, the dollar value of those sales was less than from another promotion, which could force your marketing team to redefine the desired target audience they are trying to reach.

Can Online Branding Be Measured?

According to PointRoll, branding is now the leading advertising goal in new media marketing. In fact, according to Forrester Research, 66 percent of marketing executives believe that using new media is more effective for branding than traditional marketing (Burby, April 2006). If one of your primary goals in implementing a new media campaign is strengthening your brand, does that mean you can't take advantage of tracking methods? Well, yes and no.

There are ways to track how effective your online branding is; however, doing so is less clear-cut than tracking other marketing goals such as direct sales.

The easiest way to measure the strength of your brand online is by reviewing your website traffic reports and looking at the top referrals to your site. This will tell you how people are finding your site online. If a high percentage of people are finding your website through "direct request," this can show strong name branding. Direct request means they are typing your company URL directly into the web browser, rather than finding your product or services through search engines. Another way to see how your brand measures up is by looking at the top keyword search phrases users are typing in to find your site. Do those phrases include your company name? Finally, look at the number of return visitors and repeat buyers over the course of your online branding efforts to measure the impact.

Most pay-per-click search engines provide businesses with excellent lead conversion tracking tools at no additional cost.

Measuring the Success of Search Engine Marketing

Search engine marketing is a term that encompasses search engine optimization, pay-per-click advertising, and any other way you use search engines to market your product online. The great thing about pay-per-click advertising on search engines such as Google, Yahoo! Search, and MSN is that these services actually provide you with a tracking code that you can incorporate into your website. Have your web designer put the code on the "Thank you" page of your "Contact us" form, and the "Request a quote" form, shopping cart, email list sign-up form, or any other element of your website you want to track to measure the success of the campaign. Then, you can use Google, Yahoo! Search, or MSN's tracking system to see exactly which keyword phrase leads to each conversion. Fine-tuning your search engine marketing efforts in this way can help you determine the most effective keyword phrases to optimize your site for. As you now know, optimizing your site for search engines takes time, so ensuring that you are using the right keywords before you invest time and money in the optimization process is essential.

Although the top pay-per-click search engines provide some great tracking tools, it is up to you and your marketing consultant to understand the results and act on them. In some cases, you may need to look at the big picture of the campaign in order to understand what pieces need to be modified. For example, studies have shown that branded keyword phrases generate a higher conversion rate; however, the same studies have consistently shown that generic search terms are an important piece of the research process (Sherman, May 2006). In other words, consumers use general search terms earlier in the shopping process, while they use branded terms when they are closer to making the actual purchase. Either way, for best results it is important that your company name and products consistently show up in their research path. In other words, although the branded terms may show up as more cost-effective in your marketing reports, it is important to understand that the non-branded terms often do assist in the sale.

Measuring the Success of Online PR Efforts

Online PR is an extremely effective form of new media marketing. With so many websites looking for fresh content, journalists searching for new story ideas, and search engines using link popularity as a factor in determining ranking, the use of well-thought-out and optimized press releases can be a cost-effective way to generate some great returns. However, as most marketers know, the effects of online PR, just like traditional PR, occur over a longer term. Therefore tracking the success of online PR is not as simple or clear-cut as tracking other types of online marketing elements. With that said, here are a few ways to track the success of your online PR efforts:

1. Use a service such as WebClipping.com or sign up for Google Alerts to track mentions of your company name or products online. In addition, submitting your press release through services such as PRWebDirect.com allows you to track the number of reads, forwards, printouts, and downloads of your press release. Recently, they have also started emailing useful "trackback" links showing marketers where their press releases have been picked up.

2. Check for an increase in your overall search engine ranking and/or website traffic. If you are implementing several search engine marketing strategies and new media elements all at once, it may be difficult to tell if the result of your increased search engine ranking is solely in response to a well-placed press release. However, if you are using the right website traffic software, you can tell where your

increased traffic is coming from. If you start to see some top industry or news sites popping up on your list of top referrals, you know that you are getting significant traffic from the release.

3. Use LinkPopularity.com to check how many incoming links your website has. Perhaps your recent press release has generated buzz not only in the media but on message boards and blogs. All of these links can help the overall success of your campaign.

4. Track actual media attention. Did that recent press release land you an interview on the evening news or a photo in a newspaper? Business owners know that a positive mention in a news story or editorial piece is worth much more than any paid advertisement. This type of press coverage is the most obvious way to measure the success of the campaign — and can be invaluable to your company.

5. Use your website traffic reports or pay-per-click reports to see if search terms related to your press release are driving new traffic to your site or leading to conversions.

Measuring the Success of Mobile Marketing Campaigns

Mobile marketing "metrics" are actually very similar to measuring the success of a regular Internet marketing campaign. Key areas to look at include the number of impressions, click rates, and number of conversions. Impressions refer to the number of times your ad was successfully viewed; click rates show the number of times people who viewed the ad interacted with it; and conversions are how many people who clicked the ad actually completed the desired action. In most cases with mobile marketing, the desired action is redeeming a coupon code either in a storefront or on a website.

Tracking Online Video Results

Because online video is still a relatively new advertising channel, the metrics are still fairly basic. However, even in its infancy, the effectiveness of online video is more measurable than television advertising. One way to track the success of an online video ad is by monitoring the number of times it has been seen, as well as tracking repeat views. You can also track how many times viewers forwarded the video link to a friend. This will help you determine the viral quality of the ad. You should also be able to measure the amount of time the viewer spent watching the video, or how much of the ad was viewed. If viewers continue to watch only the first few seconds, you know you need to make some modifications.

If your goal is to create a specific response, such as having viewers click to your online store, purchase a product, or sign up for an email newsletter, be sure to track those actions. It's also a good idea to track what time of day visitors watch your video and how they were referred to it. This is especially important if you are buying a number of different ads to drive traffic to your video. Knowing when and from where your viewers are coming, and which ones are taking the desired actions, will further help you refine your campaign.

Modifying Your Marketing Campaign Based on Your Results

Once you have determined your marketing goals and implemented a way to track all of the campaign elements, have a professional marketing consultant help you analyze those results. Depending on which areas need to be improved, the consultant may suggest modifying your home page, your offer, or even your overall product or price point.

New media marketing not only opens up your products and services to a larger but more targeted audience, it also allows you to quickly test new campaigns, products, and promotions before investing big money in traditional advertising channels. Think how much cheaper and faster rewording or swapping a product photo on a web page is than shooting a new television commercial; or testing a new promotion via email rather than direct mail.

Now is the time to get on board.

References

Achafer, Ian. 2006. The Case for Online Video Ratings, Revisited. *ClickZ*, May 19.

Atchison, Shane. 2006. Avoiding the Most Common Web Analytics Pitfalls. *ClickZ*, June 1.

Burby, Jason. 2006. Web Analytics and Online Branding Metrics. *ClickZ*, April 11.

____. 2006a. Web Analytics: The Delayed Conversion Concept, Part 1. *ClickZ*, May 9.

____. 2006b. Web Analytics: The Delayed Conversion Concept, Part 2. *ClickZ*, May 23.

Burns, Enid. 2006. Research: Internet Users Plagued by 'Banner Blindness.' *ClickZ*, June 26.

Cobalt/Dealix Search Marketing Team. 2005. Search Engine Marketing for Dealers. *Dealix Dealer Newsletter*, November.

Cohen, Heidi. 2006. More Than a Press Release: Extending Your Online PR Efforts. *ClickZ*, March 30.

____. 2006. How to Make Podcasting Work for You. *ClickZ*, May 25.

____. 2006. Measuring Online Video Ads. *ClickZ,* June 8.

Greenfield, Mat. 2006. Five Great Conversion Tips. *Practical Ecommerce*, July.

Lee, Kevin. 2006. Competitive Research, Intelligence, and Search Marketing, Part 2. *ClickZ*, May 5.

Marriott, Laura. 2006. Measuring WAP Ad Campaign Success. *ClickZ*, June 1.

Mason, Neil. 2006. Specialized Reporting and Analysis Tools, Part 1. *ClickZ*, May 30.

____. 2006. Specialized Reporting and Analysis Tools, Part 2. *ClickZ*, June 13.

Popov, Kirill, and Loren McDonald. 2006. Seven Steps to a Better Template. *ClickZ*, May 24.

Schmidt, Mark. 2006. Empowering Your Marketing Strategy with Decisions Mapping Tools. *Decision Tactics*, March 21.

Sherman, Chris. 2006. The Value of Branded vs. Non-Branded Search Terms. *ClickZ*, May 24.

Stelter, Phil. 2006. The Evolution of Retail and Local Search. *ClickZ*, April 27.

Stewart, Morgan. 2005. Email Marketing: 2005 Response Rate Study. http://email.exacttarget.com/ETWeb/whitepapers_form.aspx?id=466

CHAPTER ELEVEN

NEXT STEPS: PULLING IT ALL TOGETHER

Whatever your business, whether it is a start-up or an established company, the rules for developing a new media marketing plan are the same. This chapter outlines some of the core elements and costs involved in developing such a plan, along with some helpful tips for putting that plan into action.

Understand Your Target Audience

The basis of a successful Internet marketing plan (or any business plan) is understanding who your target audience is and how your company, product, or service benefits them. The more specifically you can define your target audience, the more likely you will be to develop a creative new media campaign that will produce the results you are striving for.

Once you clearly define who your customers are, you will then be able to understand how they use new media technology in their daily lives. For example, university students on a limited budget would be using the Internet differently than a working mother with a high-paying corporate job. Review Chapter 6, "Developing New Media Campaigns by Target Audience and Industry," for more help on finding your target audience online.

Identify How You Will Measure the Success of the Campaign

What are the goals of the campaign? What would make it a success? The more specific you get, the more fine-tuned your marketing campaign can be. In other words, don't just say, "I want to increase sales." Obviously the goal of any campaign is to increase the bottom line. Instead, define exactly what online elements will help you increase sales. For example, is your goal to see 10 "request a quote" forms filled out on your website every day? Or perhaps your campaign goal is to solidify your spot as a leader in the industry by attaining a number one search engine ranking for your unique products and services. Or perhaps you'd like to start building your email marketing list, with the goal of upselling to existing customers and thereby saving money on new customer acquisition costs. All of these goals require increased sales, but they give your marketing team a focused way to get those new sales.

The advantage of new media marketing is that you have the ability to track very specific actions and how they affect your overall goals. You can clearly and quickly see what's working and what's not, then make relatively low-cost changes to your website and your marketing plan until you find success. Review Chapter 10, "Measuring the Results," for more information on ways to track a new media marketing campaign for your business.

Align Your Company Goals and Values to Help Build a Stronger Online Brand

Before you begin any type of marketing campaign, you absolutely must understand the core values and overall business goals of the company. Every piece of your media campaign must not only attempt to help you reach those goals, but also be consistent with your core company values. In other words, don't create an online video or flashy website just for the sake of it. All campaign elements must help you to encourage users to take a specific action in a deliberate way as well as strengthen and differentiate your overall brand image.

Along with clearly identifying your target audience, also take some time to write down how your services or products specifically benefit your customers. In addition, define how your company differs from your competitors. These factors will most likely be the basis of your new media marketing brand. For example, perhaps your company mission statement involves offering the lowest prices. In this case, you may consider centering your campaign around downloadable coupons and free giveaways for customers who join your email list or subscribe to your "tell a friend campaign." Or perhaps you offer the best customer service, and therefore your new media campaign would center around innovative use of online support, such as live chat, tutorials (using Flash technology), or an FAQ section. Using new media technology to strengthen your core values and to stress to your company's benefits to the consumer will make your campaign more successful.

Understanding who your target audience is and how they use new media will help you know what type of website to build.

Take Time to Plan Your Website

As you enter into the new media market space, your website will be the centerpiece of the campaign. By using your website as the core of your marketing efforts, you are better able to track the results and refine your campaign. Every page of your website should encourage users to take a specific action that is aligned with your defined goals, whether it be purchasing a product, filling out a contact form, or joining your email database.

Understanding your target audience's Internet capabilities will also be key in determining the layout and structure of your website. For example, if your audience is likely to be accessing your site from work, you may want to reconsider having loud music in the introduction. Or if your company is hoping to appeal to baby boomers, you may want to ensure that your graphics and font are visually attractive to them. Again, clearly defining your audience and your goals will help you develop a website that is most likely to appeal to them. Review Chapter 8, as it contains many important elements to consider when developing your website.

Typical Costs for Implementing a New Media Campaign

Although developing and managing a new media campaign is much cheaper than conducting a national television or radio campaign, there are still some significant costs involved. Buying ad space on a major web portal can cost upwards of $15,000 USD per month. The

Advertising on a major web portal can cost upwards of $15,000 per month. However, buying ads on smaller, more targeted sites can be just as effective.

last media kit I saw from MySpace demanded a minimum ad spend of $75,000 to $250,000 for one of their integrated custom community ad buys. However, because of the very nature of the Internet — there are billions of web properties out there — with a little creative thinking you can still find some low-cost ad buy alternatives. Examples include submitting a press release or story idea to one of the major portals, or starting and managing your own MySpace page, if that is indeed where your target audience is likely to be. It is also worth looking into Google Placements. Similar to Google's traditional Adwords PPC, it allows you to place banners and text ads across hundreds of websites where your target audience is likely to be. Google Placements allows you to specify which website you want your ad to appear by topic, audience, and other specific factors and pay for those ads at a CPM or CPC rate with which you are comfortable.

Unlike traditional marketing, the Internet does still allow room for very successful marketing campaigns at very low costs. However, realistically, unless you are an ultra-tech-savvy person with lots of time on your hands and access to all the latest web development and video software, you will need to hire outside help to produce a professional campaign. Since most of us have full-time jobs specializing in one specific area, as well as deadlines we need to meet to get a new media campaign successfully off the ground, I strongly recommend hiring a full-service Internet marketing agency to help you set up and manage your campaign.

As an owner of an Internet marketing and technology consulting company, I know firsthand just how many different elements and skill sets are needed to conduct a well-rounded new media campaign. It requires not only graphic designers, web designers, and programmers, but also copywriters, search engine optimization (SEO) consultants, a hosting and technology support team, and project managers — all working together to create a seamless campaign. Prices for new media and technology consulting vary based on skill level of consultants, complexity of campaign, as well as how competitive your industry already is online.

Invest in a Professional Website

Invest in developing a quality website, just as you would invest in creating a quality storefront image or business card. Allocate about 50 percent of your marketing budget to the development of a professional website. If you must skimp on costs, save money on items such as blogs, message boards, and email marketing software. These are all items for which you can still find very cheap scripts and solutions that are relatively high quality. For example, just do a search for "free blogs" and you will find many valuable options. Most allow you to view a quick trial and easily pick and choose a layout based on the features you are most interested in. I also recommend saving money by using a third party email marketing software such as Constant Contact or iContact. It's also a good idea to ask your hosting company what type of free scripts they provide. Many hosting companies will provide customers access to excellent web traffic software and other elements to help you get your campaign off the ground at little or no additional charge. If you must, and online shopping is not your primary business goal or you only have a few products, you can also save money developing your online shopping cart by starting with a Yahoo! shopping cart or even exploring the merchant options from PayPal. As your e-commerce needs grow, you'll have a better idea of what type of custom solution and features you really need. As your company grows, you can easily upgrade these items.

Investing in a quality website design from the outset will not only help differentiate your site from the billions of websites currently trying to gain exposure in cyberspace, but more important, it will help give your company a more credible, trustworthy image overall. Consider hiring a professional web development company or even a freelance web designer with an excellent portfolio to get your website up to date and in line with your overall campaign goals. Then employ that same designer to help you brand all of your campaign elements so that you have one consistent and recognizable online brand image. Be sure to share your marketing objectives and clearly define your target audience for the web developer, so he or she can provide the best possible solution. Costs vary for development of a website based on number of pages, complexity of databases, e-commerce options, and custom graphics. Typically you can spend anywhere from $5,000 to over $25,000 for a professionally designed website.

Search Engine Marketing

Understanding the search engines and what it takes to maintain a top ranking in today's competitive world is really a full-time job. If you have the budget, I strongly recommend hiring a SEO consultant to help ensure that your website is not only optimized correctly,

It's a good idea to invest in a quick PPC campaign to ensure you are optimizing your website for the right keywords.

but optimized for the keywords that are going to help you best reach your overall campaign goals. Costs for optimizing your website and maintaining its ranking on the search engines vary, depending not only on the skill level of the SEO consultant but also on how competitive your keyword phrases are. In other words, how much effort is it going to take to transform your website into a top-ranking site for your desired keywords?

In order to educate yourself and be able to ask your SEO consultant the right questions, I suggest reviewing the search engine optimization sections detailed in Chapter 8. You can also download free trial versions of programs used by SEO consultants such as WordTracker and Web Position to help you understand the search volume for your desired keywords and where your competitors are currently ranking on the search engines.

Whether you hire a professional SEO consultant or decide to do it yourself, increasing your search engine ranking takes time. Typically, results from even the best optimization can take three months — longer if your site is brand new to the web. Therefore, I strongly recommend kicking off with a pay-per-click (PPC) campaign to find out what combination of keywords works best for your business.

Testing the Keywords before You Optimize

Before spending time and money optimizing your site for the search engines, it's a good idea to start a PPC campaign to get fast feedback on which keywords are going to work best for your site. Rather than optimizing for keywords that you *think* are going to provide you with the customers you need, then waiting three months to find out those are not the right words after all, try buying keywords first. This will not only provide instant results and trackable conversions, but will also give you an idea of which words are most expensive (i.e., valuable to your competitors). For example, rather than spending time and money optimizing your site for a keyword phrase that is only 10 cents a click, why not optimize for one of the more competitive words that are $2/click.

I recommend doing a one-month test buy on Google, Yahoo!, and MSN with more keyword phrases than you would typically buy, just to test the waters. Although Google may tend to generate the most traffic, Yahoo! or MSN may generate the most conversions. When I work with a new client, I divide their first month's PPC budget evenly three ways: one-third to Google AdWords, one-third to Yahoo! Search, and one-third to MSN Live Search. At the end of the month, we review the results to see which keywords performed the best and which PPC campaign generated the most return on investment. From this, we can refine the campaign and know which keyword combination to invest more money in, as well as which words to concentrate on for their natural search engine optimization.

Upselling to Existing Customers through Email Marketing

Unless you happen to stumble upon the perfect viral marketing plan that launches your company into record-breaking profits — such as the example of OK Go! discussed in Chapter 2 — new media plans take time and money. That's why incorporating an email marketing strategy into your plan is so important for decreasing your long-term customer acquisition costs. When done right, email marketing can help you upsell to your existing customers and help you find new customers by encouraging your already loyal customers to spread the word.

The good news is that maintaining an email marketing database can be done very inexpensively. Depending on the size of your email list and how customized you want it to be, you can typically license email marketing software such as Constant Contact or StreamSend for less than $50 per month. However, don't forget to factor in the design and copywriting costs to ensure that your message appeals to your audience and makes its way past the spam filters. I suggest reviewing the tips and CAN-SPAM Act guidelines in Chapter 9 before you send your first message.

I also suggest sitting down and planning out a year of email marketing. This will enable you to better plan for specific promotions, including any seasonal promotions you may want to do, and will make it more likely that you will adhere to a schedule. Ideally, you should be sending out some type of email communication once a month, promoting a special or offering some information that will keep customers interested in hearing from you and coming back to your website. Remember to update your home page with each promotion you are emailing out.

Strategic Partnership Development (Co-Branding)

As discussed in Chapter 7 and throughout this book, co-branding is an excellent way to launch your product into the new media by getting some leverage off a company that is already finding success in new media marketing. Start by brainstorming at least 10 products or services that would complement your product or service. For example, a web designer could team up with a hosting company; a luggage company could team up with a travel site; and so on. Think about products or services that people usually purchase together, and get creative. Then circle the top two products or services that could enhance your company's brand, reach, and credibility.

Next, think of some companies that offer those products and services that you could realistically team up with. Be sure the companies' audience and values are similar to yours and that they are interested in using new media technology to market their services. Next, brainstorm some promotions you could do with these companies, as well as the estimated costs involved in the campaign. Identify what types of services you could offer in exchange for monetary contributions. Finally, create a well-thought-out, professional proposal based on the information you have brainstormed above, clearly showing the benefits of the campaign to all parties involved. Send it to the top company you would like to partner up with. If your top choice rejects your offer, contact your second choice, and so on.

Connecting with the Customer

With new media marketing still in its infancy, your business has the opportunity to find tremendous success with a little thought, creativity, and good timing. Keep one eye on the latest Internet trends and technological advances, and think of ways your company can use that technology to better communicate its unique benefits to its audience. The whole idea behind new media marketing is using technology to better connect with your current customer base as well as to reach out to new audiences.

It wasn't long ago when a company called Netscape helped bring the World Wide Web into the mainstream. Their 1995 web browser, based on the idea of "hyperlinking," was developed using the concept that every document in the world connects to every other one in some way. This concept helped pave the way for businesses, both large and small, to find a very cost-effective way to share their products and services with a very large audience. In order to succeed in today's connected world, your company cannot live in a vacuum. Invest time in building a creative new media marketing strategy that connects you with the businesses, consumers, and community around you. In doing so, you are providing a larger pathway for business growth.